The OTHER MOTHER

JEN BRISTER

▣ SQUARE PEG

1 3 5 7 9 10 8 6 4 2

Square Peg, an imprint of VINTAGE
20 Vauxhall Bridge Road,
London SW1V 2SA

Square Peg is part of the Penguin Random House group of companies
whose addresses can be found at global.penguinrandomhouse.com

Penguin
Random House
UK

First published by Square Peg in 2019

Penguin.co.uk/vintage

A CIP catalogue record for this book is available
from the British Library

ISBN 9781910931967

Typeset in 11.5/16 pt Berling LT Std
by Integra Software Services Pvt. Ltd, Pondicherry

Printed and bound in Great Britain by Clays Ltd, Elcograf S.p.A.

Penguin Random House is committed to a sustainable future for our
business, our readers and our planet. This book is made from
Forest Stewardship Council® certified paper.

MIX
Paper from
responsible sources
FSC   FSC® C018179
www.fsc.org

The OTHER MOTHER

For my mum, for everything

In memory of Will Houghton. We miss you,
you'll always be a role model to our boys

Contents

Prologue

Whatever You Do, Don't Panic!

It wasn't my first panic attack, but just like the previous episodes, I had no idea what was happening to me. I only knew that I was about to die on a cobbled street in Edinburgh on a rainy summer's afternoon.

I was slap bang in the middle of every comedian's most traumatic month: it was August and The Edinburgh Festival. In that moment, as I sat hunched on my knees in a backstreet behind George Square, clutching my chest and gasping for breath, tears stung my eyes as I realised this *really* was it. I was dying. Accepting my inevitable fate, I looked up through my tears. A dog was taking a massive piss against the wall right in front of me. I watched the terrier's urine wending its way toward me, a meandering torrent of stinking yellow piss. Mesmerised, I could feel my heart grow calm and my breath come more easily. Struggling to my feet to dodge the dog piss, I registered with relief that, in fact, death was not on the cards for me that day. Fate had something very different in store for me.

I am thirty-nine years old. Thirty-nine. I have just bought a house I cannot afford, and frankly do not deserve, with my long-term girlfriend, Chloe. We have been together for over eight years. I am a professional stand-up comedian who probably earns less than most twenty-somethings when they graduate. I have no real concept of responsibility other than the legal require-ment to pay my utility bills and phone my mother. I frequently fail at both of these. I am thirty-nine years of age. Thirty-nine. You got that? I have no savings, career prospects or security of any kind … and in just one month's time, four weeks away from this near-death experience in a dog-piss alley in Edinburgh Old Town, I am to become a parent.

I have no real understanding of just how much my life is about to change. I failed my Adult Responsibility test, but have a PhD in arrested development and I am almost certainly not emotionally equipped to parent anything. Not even a hamster. I feel sorry for thirty-nine-year-old me.

1

Before

How did I get to be such a late bloomer and all-round permanent adolescent? You may well ask. I do. Often.

Before we go any further, we need to go back ... *back ... back ... back ...* If this was TV, at this point there'd be some eerie music and a blurry sepia tinge to let you know we're going on a flashback. But this is a book, so you'll just have to use your imagination.

To understand how I got here with my PhD in Arrested Development, we need to take a look at the young Jen Brister.

I grew up in a suburb of south-west London with my Spanish mum, my English dad and three brothers. I was number two of four, and a tomboy. I basically wanted to be like my brothers, i.e. a boy. You can imagine how delighted my mum was when her only daughter refused all the trappings that you would expect a young girl to enjoy: Care Bears, Sindy dolls, My Little Pony, dresses, even the Girl's World Styling Head left me cold. I was much happier up a tree, kicking a football about or playing bundles[1] with my brothers.

I quite liked primary school. It was a mixed school with more boys than girls. I had two best friends, neither of whom were much into the girlie stuff either. Secondary school, however, for me was like being in prison. I hated it. It was an all-girls Catholic convent school in Wimbledon. I liked the learning bit, but there always seemed to be more emphasis on telling you what you couldn't do rather than on what you could. I spent most of my time being given detention for having 'an attitude', which made no sense to me. Surely everyone has an attitude? If you don't have an attitude how can you have any opinions or viewpoints on anything? Isn't that something the school should be striving towards? More children with attitudes?

---

[1] Bundles – a game in which three of us hurled ourselves on top of the fourth. It was a lot of fun! Unless you were the person underneath.

Apparently not. Detention for me. Again.

In many ways, I was a complete idiot. In other ways I was just a lonely, flat-chested adolescent trapped so deep in the closet I might as well have moved permanently to Narnia and taken up the panpipes.

As a long-term closet resident, self-awareness wasn't my strongest point. I had about as much of that as an *X Factor* contestant murdering a Whitney Houston ballad in one of those 'worst auditions of all time' montages. That said, I had always known, even from a very young age, that I wanted to be a mum, which was confusing because I also knew that I *really* didn't want to have sex with a man.

It seems absurd now, as someone who is clearly a massive lesbo, that I ever thought that shagging a bloke could be an option for me, but let's not forget that this was the Eighties, and things couldn't have been more binary. If you were a bloke then you got with a woman and vice versa. No one was talking about being gender-fluid, non-binary or trans. Even if you were OVERTLY gay, people thought you were just a bit flamboyant. Let's not forget that there is a generation of people who still can't get their head round the fact that Liberace was gay.[2]

It's not like gay people were completely invisible in the Eighties; it's just that most people, at best, didn't

---

[2] What straight man doesn't like Cuban heels, diamanté dinner jackets and cock?

want to acknowledge them and, at worst, didn't like them. I honestly don't know how Boy George survived that decade.

So, as an adolescent at an all-girls convent school, regardless of my personal preferences, when I envisaged my future, it was with a man. When I look back at my younger self now, I find it incredible that knowing I was gay and being gay wasn't enough for me to actually come out as GAY. The years I wasted trying to like boys ...

Internalised homophobia is a truly powerful thing. I even went on a few dates, none of which ever progressed to a second, two of which stand out in particular, probably because they were so horrific. One guy took me fishing. I say fishing; he took me to the bank of the Thames where I watched *him* fish. For anyone who has ever been fishing, you'll know that NOTHING HAPPENS. After being bored out of my mind watching him run his fingers through a bucket of maggots for two hours, he went in for a kiss. I panicked, and punched him in the chest, causing him to step backwards into the river. You may judge my reaction a tad harsh, but the guy was wearing Wellington boots *on a date*!

My last ever date with a boy was when I was fifteen. He was in the sixth form, which made him glamorous. Slightly less glamorous was his idea of a great night out: he took me to McDonald's because he had two sets of vouchers for a McChicken Sandwich and a lemonade. If I was lucky, maybe he'd buy me a side order of regular fries. I never saw the fries, but later that afternoon I did get to watch him play *Double Dragon* for two hours in a kebab shop in New Malden. Someone, shoot me in the face.

I gave up any attempt at cultivating a liking for boys after that, but I still had no real understanding about lesbians – there just weren't any around, either in my life or on TV. In fact, the only film I'd ever seen involving any lesbians was *The Killing of Sister George* and frankly the image of the terrifyingly predatory and drunk Beryl Reid in her bosomy tweeds wasn't much help on the lezza role-model front. If you're not represented by the media and have never met anyone like you, then you start to think that you might be the only one. After all, none of my friends seemed to be questioning who they were attracted to, or whether or not it was normal to fancy Stefanie Powers in *Hart to Hart* and Lynda Carter's *Wonder Woman* and Lisa Stoddart ... and Julie Wilson, and Claire Bright and Hannah Ainsworth and that girl with a ponytail two years above me and that girl that worked in a cafe on Kingston High Street ... Oh God. All teenage girls fancy girls, don't they?

Time went on. I left school, I went to university. I was happy enough with my life, but I was missing certain landmarks. Unsurprisingly, I never had a boyfriend.

In fact, I couldn't imagine having a relationship with anyone; it seemed like something other people did. But I knew that I wanted children. Even as a single closeted twenty-something, I continued to have dreams about being a mum.

In one dream, I gave birth to a baby girl. She just slipped out. (IT WAS A DREAM, OK?) I felt an intense love for this tiny daughter, but after a short while I noticed that something wasn't quite right, she was slightly deformed. I turned to my mum in the dream and said, 'Mum, one of her bum cheeks is bigger than the other!' My mother looked at me and said, 'Don't worry, it will drop eventually.'

What can I say? I like cheese before bedtime.

In real life, there was the quandary as to how I could get pregnant without having any actual involvement with a man. How did I imagine these children would arrive? By carrier pigeon? What's more, I have no idea how I thought I could possibly have taken responsibility for raising a child back then. I couldn't even take responsibility for myself.

My twenties were a chaotic and directionless mess. I look at twenty-somethings now who seem so together and level-headed and I think, 'How do you know what you're doing?' I spent twelve years bouncing from one job I hated to another, with no plan for the future. I didn't get my shit together even after I came out of my oh-so cosy closet. Yeah, I know you'd think that that was the problem! And maybe it was. I never had a traditional adolescence after all, and so in my late twenties, I decided to stretch mine out for as long as possible.

Arrested development is a trait that many gay men and women of my generation nurtured over many years, believe me; but if you're in any doubt, go to your local Gay Pride march and take a look around you. In fact, forget that, go to Brighton Pride. Honestly, it's not unusual to see a sixty-five-year-old man wandering around the Co-Op dressed as a Roman centurion with his arse hanging out. No one bats an eyelid. Try doing that as a straight man at your summer fete and you *will be* arrested.

My chosen career as a stand-up comedian didn't help either – if there was ever a group of people with a Peter Pan complex it's circuit comics. The job just doesn't lend itself to a personality that enjoys security, routine or any semblance of normality. As a comedian, you spend your life on the road travelling from one gig to another, working when everyone else is out having a good time. You inhabit a world in which your success is far from guaranteed, your future is uncertain and where other people's successes can feel like they detract from your own. You spend your days thinking about how you can get more work, better work, write more, do more, scratch and scrape your way to the next level. You are basically riding on a heady cocktail of adrenaline and delusion. In short, you are a self-obsessed wanker.

Most of my life had felt out of control, like I was flying by the seat of my pants. Something had to change.

2

Decisions, Decisions

My singlehood had stretched from adolescence to university. I had managed to delay coming out of the closet until I was twenty-two and when I finally did fall in love, I was convinced it would be forever.

When that first relationship unsurprisingly ended, after four years, I found myself emotionally ill-equipped to date women. I may have been in my late twenties but I had the emotional maturity of a four-teen-year-old boy.[1]

Single again, I went a bit bonkers trying to make up for lost time. The problem was that I wanted to have fun, but I discovered that I'm not really someone who

---

[1] Think Dustin in *Stranger Things*.

does 'fun' very well. I started to date women 'casually', and quickly discovered that the 'casual' part existed only in my head. I'd go out with these women, go through all the motions, but spend the entire time thinking: 'I wonder when would be the best moment to end this? I can't dump her today, it's her birthday.' The problem was that no matter how casual it was in my mind, you can't hang out with someone and sleep with them for months on end and 'not be' in a relationship, apparently. For any single straight men reading this,[2] listen up: it doesn't matter how many times you say the word 'casual', a lot of women have this crazy way of ignoring the words that come out of your mouth and judging you entirely on your actions.

After four hedonistic years of going to queer club nights and bouncing from one short term non-relationship to the next, I met Chloe.

How to describe Chloe? In brief, let's just say that Chloe is a woman with a steady and successful career and a family who all get on – they love spending time together, never really argue and no one ever divorces. They are basically the Waltons recast in the Home Counties. She has a savings account, with actual savings in it, a pension and owns her own property.

Obviously, when such a woman meets a jobbing stand-up career adolescent with no whiff of a livelihood,

[2] IT IS POSSIBLE.

an overdrawn overdraft and a family with a long heritage in dysfunction (that's me, by the way), it is an inevitability that she fall for her, head over heels and hook, line and sinker.[3]

I would love to say that entering into a long-term relationship gave me the stability I needed to pursue my career in comedy in earnest. The truth, however, was that Chloe was as confused about her feelings for me as I was about my future; until she met me, she had considered herself 'straight' and would spend the next five years trying to get her head round the fact that she fancied women, or at least *a* woman (that's still me).

The chaos continued until I turned thirty-six. There's something about reaching that age that made me take stock. At thirty you're still close to being in your twenties, you also have the energy of someone in your twenties, but at thirty-six, you're only four years away from forty – and we all know that forty is *old*. (Unless, like me, you actually are forty,[4] in which case, UP YOURS! Forty is not old. Forty is the new thirty, you total bell!)

During my thirties, as my career took hold, the dream of being a parent had begun to recede somewhat

---

[3] Yes, I am genuinely amazed as well.
[4] OK, in the spirt of full disclosure, I'm actually forty-four. Moving on swiftly …

and by my thirty-sixth birthday, it seemed far from the realm of possibility. Then, around this same time, Chloe decided that we should probably live together. Again. We had tried cohabitation briefly just a year earlier, but Chloe had panicked and asked me to move out. Ha-ha! Good times. We're over it now, and you know what? Being homeless isn't the worst thing that can happen to you, or so Chloe kept assuring me.

So, I moved back in with Chloe and we hadn't been living together very long before the subject of children started to crop up in our conversation. Most of it went a bit like this:

'I really want to have children, but I also just really like my life as it is.'

'Me too. Kids would be great, but I do really love sleeping.'

'I would love a baby.'

'Yeah, so would I ...'

'But not right now ...

'God no! Not now. We've got three weddings to go to. I can't be sober for them.'

'Yeah. No fun, and I've always wanted to learn to rollerblade.'

'Maybe in a couple of years when we're ready.'

If I was really honest with myself, I had to admit that I was now far from certain that I definitely wanted kids. Not all women want kids, after all. In much the same way that we don't all wear make-up, read *Cosmo* or wear tights. (I hate tights, I will never wear tights again as long as I live. They make your feet sweat in the summer and your feet freeze in the winter. And what's with the gussets that force you to waddle like you've just deposited a load in your pants?)

At this point we were two carefree thirty-somethings living in north London. I was travelling the world with stand-up and Chlo had established herself in self-employment and was enjoying the autonomy it gave her. We had a nice life. We had friends we could hang out with regularly, we enjoyed our Saturday morning lie-ins and late breakfasts, walks on Hampstead Heath and the occasional weekend away when I was strong-armed into taking time off. In short, life was sweet.

Not sweet enough apparently.

In our case, Chloe was always the one with a life plan: fast-forward a year after I'd moved in and she had convinced me that what we were actually doing was running out of time. We were ready, we told ourselves, to have a child.

Ready? READY? Who the hell is ready? The answer is NO ONE. I really don't think people put enough thought into what being a parent might entail. It's a huge decision, it's a ridiculous decision to say yes to, it's a decision that most of us are not equipped to make. Because what you are in fact deciding to do is give up a big chunk of you, who you are, your freedom, your identity, your LIFE! In the case of me and Chloe, let's just say that I can't emphasise enough how unready we were.

For a start, we hadn't even discussed when, where or how we were to acquire said 'child'.

There are loads of upsides to being a lesbian: not giving a flying fuck what men think is one of them, but the main one is that you never have to worry about getting up the duff. If you're a gay woman you're not going to get pregnant by 'accident', which is GREAT! Until you want to get pregnant, then being a lesbian is a massive ball ache, or should I say, womb ache.

That's not to say we didn't have choices. Of course we did. We just hadn't really thought them through, or properly had that conversation. For a short while, I just assumed that adoption would probably be the way to go. I know adoption isn't for everyone: there is no doubt that it's a big responsibility to take on a child or children that may have complex needs and/or emotional issues. Adopting a child can be challenging. It also doesn't help that while the system has been streamlined, it can still be bureaucratic and slow. Saying all of that, we had witnessed our friends' journey after they adopted a two-year-old boy, slowly but surely becoming a strong family unit, and it was truly heart-warming. (And this is coming from one of the most relentlessly cynical people you'll ever meet.)

I'll be honest with you, the thought of adopting made me feel kind of smug in a liberal do-the-right-thing kind of way. After all, giving a child who needs it a home, security and love is the right thing to do. Future me would easily be able to provide a child with that! ANGELINA JOLIE, EAT YOUR BLOODY HEART OUT! I don't know why I wasn't being given some kind of prize for altruistic daydreaming.

I was in a relationship, though, and how to become a family was not a decision I could take on my own. Cue conversation with Chloe:

'What do you think about adoption?'

'I think it's great ...'

'Good, 'cos I've looked into it and—'

'Why don't we see if we can get pregnant first?'

'I'm thirty-seven! I don't think I can get preg—'

'Good. I'll do it then. I think I'd be jealous if you were pregnant anyway.'

It's that kind of relationship of equals that most people can only dream of.

Chloe wanted to try to have a baby and I totally respected that choice. The drive for human beings to procreate is primal; I'd be lying if I said that urge completely passed me by. Let's not forget my vivid dreams of babies with one large buttock. But on the whole, I really don't care. Continuing my genes means very little to me, but being a parent does. There is no shame in admitting that biology is important; equally if, like me, you don't give a toss, then adoption is a great option. Had Chloe not felt a longing to be pregnant I like to think we would have adopted a child, but as with all the most important decisions in your life, you have to be true to yourself. Having a baby mattered for Chloe, so pregnancy it was to be.

Chloe needed to have a fertility test, so she visited her local GP. So far so good. Her doctor asked her the usual routine questions, one of which was how long she had been trying for a baby and how often she was having sex. When Chloe explained that her partner was in fact, me, a woman, her GP's response was to laugh in her face and say, 'You can't get pregnant with a woman, you do realise that?' Angry and humiliated, Chloe responded. 'Actually, you can. It's called IVF, so just give me the test.'

It's unbelievable really that some GPs can still discount gay men and gay women by assuming that all relationships are heterosexual, thus making gay people feel invisible. It doesn't take much for a doctor or nurse to ask the question as to who your partner is. Perhaps a bit of unconscious bias training wouldn't go amiss.

After having the fertility test, Chloe's results didn't exactly fuel us with confidence. So, after hours of research and any number of conversations with anyone who could offer sound advice, we decided to sidestep

IUI (intrauterine insemination) and go straight to IVF (in vitro fertilisation).

Then there was the small practicality of my finances. I was completely skint and if we were going to try IVF it was going to cost money. A LOT of money.

Even though I was thirty-seven by the time we finally got our heads round the fact that we were really going to go for it, I was still desperately trying to scratch a decent living from stand-up. It wasn't like I wasn't working, I was working ALL THE TIME! I just didn't seem to be making that much money. Naturally, I had no savings; in fact, forget savings – I hadn't been in the black for longer than a day since I left university. Yeah, you heard me right: I had more money when I was a student than I had then. No one could say that Chloe was with me for my money. In any relationship there's always going to be one of you who earns more money at any given time. This can sometimes prove challenging, particularly at the beginning of a relation-ship when you have to negotiate the things you can and can't do together because of your budget. But once you've settled into a 'committed' relationship you might decide to pool your money together. After all, we're in this for the long haul and your money is my money. Right? Riiiiiight?

This is what Chloe and I had decided to do and it was working out really well (for me), other than a few passive-aggressive conversations:

'I just think you should consider doing a PGCE.'

'FOR THE LAST TIME, I DO NOT WANT TO TEACH!'

'Maybe you could combine comedy with teaching ... ?'

'Aaaaaaargh!'

We had basically nailed communication and relationships. It turns out, they're easy when you're not really listening and just doggedly pursuing what you want to do with no real thought for the future.

If you think you're judging us now ... strap yourself in.

3

Try, Try & Try Again

The thing about having children with the person you love is that you get to create a family between you. If conceiving 'naturally', it's the age-old recipe: introduce your egg to their sperm, thoroughly mix to combine DNA to the right consistency, and voila! You have made another human being! When you think about it, that is pretty bloody crazy. You can look at your child and say to yourselves:

'She has your eyes!' Or, 'He has your knees!'[1]

You can feel smug in the knowledge that the future of your genes is tied up in a perfect, neat little package; your baby. And all you needed to do to create

---

[1] I'm not sure if that's a thing or not.

that bundle of joy was to have a bout of good old-fashioned sex.

Lucky you.

Obviously, I'm exclusively referring to the heteros out there. This baby-making stuff is a breeze for most of you.[2] For many straight couples, planning for a baby merely involves not using contraception. (Look, I know I'm making a generalisation here, I also know that plenty of heterosexual couples struggle to get pregnant, but those couples aren't helping me make this point so I've chosen to ignore them.)

For gay couples it's not quite so straightforward. Gay men have the biggest challenge because they need to find a woman to carry and give birth to their child. For gay women it's a bit easier, all we need to do is find a sperm donor, and how hard can that be? After all, there's gallons of the stuff, right?

When I say that I do mean in sperm banks, not just random containers of jizz lying around your home and office. Although if men could get away with it, believe me there'd be jam jars full all over the place ...

'Sarah, do you know where the tea is?'

'Yeah, it's just behind that large bottle of spaff.'

I'm giving men a lot of credit here, the idea that they'd go to the trouble of bottling it is absurd.

'John, why is this tea towel rock solid?'

---

[2] Not ALL OF YOU! I know that.

My point is, if you're a gay woman and you want to get hold of some sperm, panic not, because you can. Almost every clinic has a sperm bank attached to it or at least one that they can recommend and if you can't find anything there that you like the look of, panic not, because there are loads more of them! Honestly, just google it.

No, the difficulty isn't finding sperm; it's the overwhelming availability of choice that is the problem. You could lose half your life scouring through all the options. Tall men, short men, fat men, thin men. Men with hair, men without. Students, surgeons, skydivers, and everything in between. Caucasian men. Black men. Asian men. South-East Asian men. Athletic men, intellectual men, funny men, boring men. Men, men, men, men! I have never taken so much interest in so many different men in my entire life.

If you're still confused as to what the hell is going on here, let me explain, because on the face of it, it sounds like I've met a lot of men, assessed their physical and intellectual assets, and chosen their sperm accordingly.

No.

You don't meet anyone (it's pretty much anonymous), in fact you don't even get to see anyone's face, so, you have no actual idea what your donor looks like. The information you do get also varies from sperm bank to sperm bank. We considered a few but eventually chose our sperm bank purely on the basis of how much information they gave. We wanted as much as possible. The criteria that you use to help you choose a donor can be anything from nationality, skin tone, hair colour, height, build, interests, hobbies, career, dick size[3] ... it's like a dating website except you're not allowed any contact with the chosen man, but you *are* allowed their sperm to create a baby. It's all very normal.

Our chosen sperm bank provided a photo of the potential donors as a baby, a letter and a recording of them talking about who they are, their hobbies etc., so we could get an idea of their personality, which is code for checking they're not a complete douche.

So, armed with this information and a choice of donor, now all we had to do was pick which one would provide 50 per cent of our prospective baby's DNA. No drama, should be pretty straightforward, right?

Not really, no.

Some sperm banks may only have a couple of hundred donors, which sounds like a lot, but if you're looking for the perfect match, that can be quite a small pool to pick from.

Maybe you want your donor to be a tall musician with an interest in the arts, creative but also intellectual, kind, attractive, curious, happy, with a good career

[3] Kidding! But I think it would be good to know.

and a sense of humour, along with olive skin and a full head of hair …

Well, good luck finding that bloke.

Lord knows we tried.

If we did find a donor that we liked the sound of, inevitably there was no sperm left, or on looking at his family history we'd discover that every woman in his family had breast cancer or his grandparents and parents had dementia.

We spent days, weeks, maybe more, trying to pick the ideal 50 per cent of our baby's gene pool. I don't know if it usually takes this long for other couples, but what I will say is that the longer you take to pick a donor, the harder it becomes to pick a donor.

With hindsight my criteria clearly illustrated my own neurosis about being the 'other mother' at the time. I think I was secretly trying to find a donor who most matched me: in other words, someone with my half-Spanish olive skin, stunning good looks and (what I vainly liked to think of as) my artistic Latin temperament.

'Shall we see if we can find a Spanish donor?'

'Yeah, that's a great idea! OK … let's look … here's one … oh, no. He's only five foot six.'

'What if we have a boy and he's only five foot four? Just search under olive skin …'

'What about this guy? Let's look at his baby photo.'

'Oh my God, he's boss-eyed!'

'Some babies are boss-eyed and then their eyes straighten out.'

'I'm not having a boss-eyed kid. Next!'

'How about this one?'

'He likes shooting and fast cars. What a bellend.'

And so it went on.

Now, of course I realise that my selection process was bonkers. The idea that if we chose a donor with olive skin then we might have a baby who looked like me was absurd. We are *two women*! It's not like anyone was going to think we created a baby together, for crying out loud.

Well, you'd think that but actually the number of people who have said this to me:

'He looks just like you.'

'I don't think he does.'

'I know you're not genetically related, but he looks JUST LIKE YOU!'

It's true, he does look a bit like me and it's mainly because he has OLIVE SKIN! So, it did work! Ha!

I digress, because at this point, we still hadn't chosen anybody's sperm and it was keeping us up at night. Choosing sperm was even harder than trying to agree on what to watch together on Netflix.

We started with so many high ideals of what we wanted. Chloe wanted him to be able to play the guitar and be creative, I wanted him to have a high IQ and beige skin, we both wanted him to be tall, athletic, fun. It was also important that he be open to having contact with our child, should he/she decide they wanted to do that in the future. Every donor can opt in or out of being contacted and I can completely understand why you wouldn't want that. There's quite a large chasm between jizzing into a cup and meeting your offspring. However, it was really important to both of us that our child would be able to have contact with their donor if they needed or wanted to. And for the record the donor is the donor, not a father. A father is someone who is actively involved in bringing up a child, not someone who is paid for their semen.

Another thing we had to bear in mind was that we were obviously not the only couple using this donor's sperm. Our child would potentially have a dozen or more half-brothers and -sisters around the world. The sperm bank we had chosen had an international reach and each donor could have a maximum of twenty-five offspring.

I KNOW!

What you can quite easily forget is that there are multiple families using the same donor as you and many of those families are having more than one child so if you have chosen a 'popular' donor the chances are this guy will already have *a lot* of children.

This is something you have to reconcile if you're going to go down this route because there's a chance (albeit a small one) that your son or daughter might meet a half-sibling without knowing it, maybe fall in love, have lots of incestuous sex, start a family and then realise they're actually siblings!

(Yes, this is an actual conversation that Chloe and I have had. We agreed that the only way to deal with the horror of such an outcome is to not acknowledge this reality and never speak of it again. So far, it's working really well.)

Eventually we did manage to narrow our choices down to three and to this day I can't say definitively why we chose the donor we did. All I can tell you is that it was one of the hardest decisions Chloe and I have ever had to make as a couple (and I was allowed to help choose our sofa[4]). In the end, I think we were so worn down by the whole process we just forced ourselves to decide, and what was it that swayed us? Well, you get a note from the clinic staff who give you a couple of lines with their impression of the donor and the response to our final choice was this:

'This guy is so hot and everyone in the clinic fancies the pants off him. Basically, if I was going to rate him out of two, *I would give him ONE!*'

OK, they didn't explicitly say that, we were both just reading between the lines, but that was the general gist.

---

[4] That's a lie, Chloe picked it up secondhand, but I didn't say we couldn't have it, so that's almost the same thing.

Once we'd agreed on our chosen donor, we seemed to forget that he wasn't that tall, or creative, and that he sounded a bit arrogant in his recording. On the plus side, he had a really cute baby photo, he was beige and he could play the guitar.

At some point I know we are going to have to answer questions about how we came to the decision and I for one cannot wait to have those discussions:

'Well, your mum and I spent a long time trying to find the perfect person to make you, my darling.'

'How did you choose him? Is he clever? Is he athletic? Does he love music like I do?'

'I don't know, love, I just know that two women in a sperm bank in Seattle thought he was really hot. I hope that helps.'

The reality is that you're never going to pick the perfect donor and it almost doesn't matter because the little bundle that comes out the other end will be your baby and you'll love them no matter what. And you will often look at them and completely forget that you're not *technically* related, because they are yours, and even if they are vertically challenged, love guns and cars and have a boss-eye, to you they will be nothing short of perfect.

But first there was the IVF to deal with ...

Trying to have a baby is in many ways such an elusive concept, because until something actually happens and you conceive, you're just shagging. Or in our case hanging out in a fertility clinic waiting room watching *Homes Under the Hammer*, trying to avoid eye contact with someone who looks like they might want to strike up a conversation about their fibroids.

In our excitement at the prospect of impending parenthood we had told everyone we knew that we were trying for a baby. Of all the rookie mistakes to make. If I can offer anyone trying for a baby advice, it's this, DON'T TELL ANYONE. Unless they are actually someone that you want to have endless conversations with about your fertility, ovulation and how their cousin got pregnant when she least expected it and don't worry it will happen if you just relax. Great, thanks, mate, I'll pass that on to my girlfriend.

'Just relax, love, you'll get pregnant in no time!'

Poor Chloe. It made me want to scream: 'Is this conversation relaxing enough for you? Are you finding the endless injections, pessaries, visits to the clinic and hormonal devastation RELAXING?'

As a gay couple, it was going to take more than some mindfulness and a sexy massage to get Chloe up the duff. As the 'other mother', my skills as all-round Teasmade, appointment buddy and lavender oil foot-rubber was about the only role I could play in this process, though. I was increasingly the spare part in our quest to become a family.

Trying to get pregnant can be an emotional roller-coaster. Yes, of course it can happen first time for some cisgender women and trans men, but it can also be a long, painful and lengthy process that saps all the emotional energy from both partners. If you're in any doubt as to the truth of that statement then I suggest you try hanging out in a fertility clinic for a couple of hours to soak in the tension and taste just a fraction of the all-out desperation.

I appreciate that IVF is an emotive process and there are no guarantees but the first clinic we went to was *truly awful*. At the start of our treatment they told us little to nothing about what was going on, what the drugs were for and what alternatives there might be if we didn't get pregnant.

The first step was to get eggs from Chloe which were then fertilised with the donor sperm. The resulting embryos were not of a grade that was *ever* going to be workable. Suddenly the clinic turned communicative and told us as much, but even though the chances of getting pregnant were therefore less than zero, for some inexplicable reason that didn't stop them putting us through a round of embryo implantation. It was as if they thought they might as well stick them up Chloe's chuff, because WHAT'S A GRAND BETWEEN FRIENDS?

They were a bunch of cowboys who took our money, offered a below par service and then ignored us to the point that it almost started to become funny. The truth is it would have been funnier still if we'd simply placed the money that we gave them in their waiting room bin, and set it on fire.

Needless to say, we didn't get pregnant. It's fine. I've let it go now and I hold absolutely no resentment in my heart for those unscrupulous, thieving bastards.

Admittedly it didn't help that we had pinned a lot of hope on it being successful. But this was definitely compounded by the fact that the tossers at that clinic made us feel like we were deluded to think we could ever get pregnant. We left feeling demoralised and depressed and angry. Did I mention I was angry?

The great thing about anger is that it can be quite the motivator, so, bruised but not yet broken, we set out to find a new clinic, one that would be a little more empathetic in their approach.

The second clinic was in Chelsea, where we had our first meeting with our doctor in a windowless box-room. I liked him immediately, although as with many people in the medical profession he had the bedside manner of a wooden spoon:

'Can I ask how old you are?'

'Me? I'm thirty-seven …'

'Oh no, no. I don't think so. How about you?'

'Thirty-five.'

'That's a bit better. Let's go with you.'

People have trouble believing that he was so blunt, but that is exactly what he said. I had had no desire to get pregnant until our doctor uttered those words and I was unceremoniously dismissed. I felt less offended than defensive.

'Listen, mate,' I felt like saying, 'I may be thirty-seven years young but I have the eggs of a twenty-five-year-old. How do I know that?' (Momentary pause.) 'I don't. And it's this kind of clueless ignorance that has fed the overly confident and deluded lezza you see before you today.'

Obviously, I didn't say anything like that. What I actually said was, 'Fair enough.'

There was something about our new doctor's direct approach that I found refreshing. With him, at least we knew were we stood. Well, sort of. The fact is, you never really know where you stand when you're dealing with fertility. You learn very soon that looking for any reassurance from a fertility clinic is like expecting a coherent answer from Mystic Meg.

Our doctor was master of the gnomic response to all but the most straightforward questioning and even though our overall experience was very positive, I started referring to him in private as Dr Seuss. Here's a taster conversation:

'So, what are the chances of getting pregnant this time round?'

'Well, we like to be positive but of course we can't say definitively if you will or won't get pregnant.'

'No, of course not, but percentage-wise, would you say it's quite high?'

'We don't like to attribute percentages, but if we did, you'd be looking at the average percentile which is not as low as you think.'

'I see ...'

'We do have a number of tests you could try, although we can't say they'll help.'

'Do you think we should take these tests?'

'You could take them for peace of mind.'

'OK, how much are they?'

'Each test will be anything from six hundred pounds.'

'But you can't say if we need them.'

'You might need them, but we won't know that until you take them.'

At times, the inevitable obfuscation was frustrating. It was round about this point in the undertaking that we began to realise that IVF is not an exact science. In fact, it sometimes crossed my mind that they didn't really know what the hell they were doing. It was so frustrating and exhausting, so much money and heartache was at stake, yet the whole process felt about as precise as watching two toddlers play Velcro darts while blindfolded.

With every new round of IVF Chloe was having to contend with an entire medicine cabinet of different drugs, each with its own very special side effect.

'Don't be alarmed if you feel like bursting into tears for no reason at all, that's very common.'

'I think I'll be fine.'

'It's not unusual to have mood swings, bouts of depression, irrational thoughts, headaches, blurred vision, nausea, bloating, dizziness and even hot flushes.'

'Honestly, I think I'll be OK.'

Fortunately for us, Chloe doesn't really do feelings. She wasn't being blasé; the woman has the constitution of a block of granite. She never gets ill, she rarely if ever gets emotional – unless you count watching the marathon and *X Factor*. That's when the floodgates open with Chloe:

'Are you OK?'

'I just think it's so amazing that all these people are running for charity! This man only has one leg and this woman is partially blind! And they're still RUNNING!'

Who knew that people running en masse was going to be such an emotional trigger? To be honest, it was a relief because I was starting to think I might have fallen for a living breathing robot.

She was taking drugs to suppress her menstrual cycle, drugs to stimulate her ovaries, drugs to stop her from ovulating early and finally drugs to thicken the lining of her womb. One evening as I watched her swallow another delicious handful of pills, I asked her how she was feeling.

'Fine,' she replied.

I've suffered harsher side effects from eating unpasteurised cheese.

To be honest, it might have helped if she *had* felt a bit nuts, if there had been some kind of external sign that she was going through something. At least that way I could have felt a bit more involved.

Increasingly, being the 'other' parent was a weird position to be in. No matter how committed you are to 'the process' or to your partner, when you're not the one trying to get pregnant it's hard to stay 100 per cent connected, twenty-four hours a day. There is a disconnect with what is happening to your partner (everything) and what is happening to you (absolutely nothing). Naturally, I think, a little part of your brain will start to shut down, or at least a bit of mine did. In truth, for someone who considers herself pretty empathetic there were times during the endless IVF process where I was completely disengaged.

Of course, I made sure I attended every single appointment at the clinic but even so I started to feel guilty about the fact that I was only ever partially participant at any given meeting. I would sit there with a face that seemed fully engrossed, but a lot of the time I was thinking about what I was going to have for lunch or whether or not I'd sent off that invoice. I'm not relaying this with any pride. I tried to be 'present' during my girlfriend's IVF treatment and be supportive, and I think for the most part I was, but my point is that I simply wasn't really essential to the entire proceedings. Any of the proceedings. I felt dispensable.

The more I became invested in the idea of becoming a parent, the more I grew aware that anything I did or didn't do would not, and could not, affect the final outcome. If there was a graph that charted my increasing obsession with wanting Chlo to get pregnant alongside how utterly useless I increasingly felt, it would be the perfect visual illustration. Unfortunately, I don't understand PowerPoint, so you'll have to imagine it.

I didn't talk to anyone about how I was feeling. It didn't seem relevant and no one asked. Why would they? I wasn't the one who had to go under general anaesthetic to have my eggs removed, who had to inject myself with numerous drugs, be poked and prodded, and endure countless blood tests. I was just there, hanging around, waiting expectantly and hoping for the best. It's not as if my sperm was involved, because I don't have sperm. I'm clearly a woman, no matter what the toilet attendant in Cobham Services thinks.

Even if you consider yourself to be the most pragmatic, dispassionate and objective person on the planet, the process of trying for a baby is all consuming. Once started, we very quickly realised that the stakes were stratospherically high. The imagined baby suddenly became our everything. It didn't seem to matter that just a few months before we had been perfectly happy without a baby, that we enjoyed our jobs, our friends, our social life, our independence. Now all we wanted was a baby, with no real understanding of what having a baby meant.

You'd think, given how complicated it is to actually get pregnant as a same sex couple, we would have really put some thought into what being a parent actually might entail. I'm not saying we didn't put in *any* thought, I'm just saying it might not have been the *right* kind …

'I wonder if we'll have a boy or a girl …'

'I hope it's a girl.'

'I *hope* it's a boy!'

'I can't wait to buy tiny little baby grows!'

'I can't wait to see what he or she looks like!'

'It's going to be so amazing!'

Dear God. What a pair of pillocks.

On occasion, however, my daydreaming took a less optimistic turn. Sometimes walking back from the clinic to the Tube station I was overcome by the overwhelming feeling that it wasn't going to happen for us. We'd left it too late. We were both too old. I tried to tell myself that whatever happened maybe it was for the best. Maybe I could reconcile a life without children – after all, it wasn't like we were unhappy together with our lot.

What's more, I told myself, if Chloe did get pregnant, by the time the baby was born I'd be nearly forty. When our child got to my age I'd be nearly eighty! Jesus, whichever way you spin it, that's properly old. Our yet-unconceived child was going to be burdened with ancient parents just at the point when they should be enjoying their own lives/family/career. Weren't we just being selfish? After all, we didn't need to have children, the world is overpopulated as it is. We could still adopt!

Deep down, though, I knew Chloe and I weren't ready to stop trying. We were both in it for the long haul.

Time was not on our side. We had started IVF when Chloe was thirty-five. Now she was nearly thirty-seven and this eighteen-month period had felt like we were in limbo. We had run out of money and if this cycle of IVF treatment failed, we knew that neither of us could face the prospect of going through the process again for a third time. Waiting to find out what shape this second batch of embryos was in was tense; if this lot weren't up to scratch our chances of getting pregnant were very low.

We sat opposite Dr Seuss in anticipation of his next riddle.

'I'm happy to say we have a number of blastocyst embryos and I'd be very surprised if you didn't get pregnant this time.'

'What? Did you just say that you'd be surprised if we *didn't* get pregnant? DID YOU JUST SAY THAT? SAY IT AGAIN, DOC. THIS TIME SPELL IT OUT AND SIGN IT IN MAKATON!'

Of course, I didn't say that. I just stared at Chloe in dumbfounded silence. Dr Seuss was no longer talking in tongues and the news was finally good!

We were going to be parents!

On the morning of that all-important pregnancy test we stared at that plastic wand for a very long time.

'What do you think that is? Do you think it's a cross … ?'

'Erm … It looks like a sort of half cross. Does it have to be a whole cross?'

'Maybe it starts as a half cross and becomes a whole cross …'

'Pee on it again.'

'It won't make any difference.'

'I think it needs more pee.'

'YOU PEE ON IT THEN!'

Six weeks and one scan later and any pregnancy that may have existed had gone.

It's hard to stay positive when you're told that you should be pregnant and you're not.

'Yes, we were surprised that one didn't stick but there are a number of tests you could take which might explain why this is happening.'

GIVE. ME. STRENGTH.

We knew something had to be wrong because Chlo had produced five blastocyst embryos. These are embryos that are at least five to seven (rather than three) days old and mean the chances of getting pregnant are a lot higher. It also means that after they are frozen, they have a much higher chance of surviving the thaw. But we had already lost one, which was odd if not completely out of the ordinary, and the only way to find out was to blow a load more money on a load more tests.

Or, thanks to yours truly, just one more test. Up until this point I'd felt about as much use as a chocolate teapot, but finally I was allowed to shine. Dr Seuss listed all the different reasons why Chloe might be struggling to stay pregnant. It was possible that her immune system was attacking the embryo, assuming it to be a foreign body. If anyone's immune system was going to go on the attack it was Chloe's. I knew that if we were going to spend £500 on a random test it had to be this one. Am I right, or am I right?

Yes, I was right. Thanks for asking.

Let's just say that Chloe was reluctant to take a test that cost £500 and that might or might not prove useful. BUT I convinced her because when necessary I can be very pushy and also, it wasn't my money.

That aside, I was correct, and after a course of steroids that would normally floor most people, my girlfriend turned into some kind of turbo-charged version of herself.

'It's six a.m. Why aren't you up? Let's go for a run! I FEEL SO ALIVE!!!!!'

Several weeks later, we were ready for the new embryo to be transferred. I say 'embryo' ...

'I want to put two embryos in.'

'I think that's a bad idea, Chlo. Remember what the doctor said, if we put two in, we might have twins and I don't think we can handle twins.'

'What does he know? He said we'd get pregnant last time and we didn't.'

'I think we should just start with one embryo and see how we go.'

'No, I want to put both in and then at least one of them will stick.'

'But what if both of them stick?'

'Then we get two for one! Bargain.'

'But I kind of don't want ...'

'I'm doing it.'

'OK.'

With hindsight, transferring two embryos was pretty cavalier, but even I had to concede that we'd got this far, so we might as well go for broke. Right?

The morning Chloe took this next pregnancy test felt very different to our previous IVF attempts. We both felt positive and, dare I say, upbeat.

'Wow! That is definitely a cross.'

'I think that cross took steroids.'

'I am very, very pregnant.'

Chloe was indeed very, VERY pregnant.

4

Up the Duff

It's great being pregnant, particularly when you're not the one that's pregnant. I don't think there can be a greater level of smugness in the entire world.

One of the benefits of not being pregnant, but having a partner who is, seems to be how perfectly normal it is for couples to announce, 'We're pregnant!' As if that's a thing. Don't think for a second that I didn't jump on that bandwagon. I would enter rooms, take centre stage and exclaim, 'Look at us! *We* are pregnant!'

We weren't pregnant, Chloe was pregnant; I was just standing next to a pregnant woman announcing a joint pregnancy that didn't exist. Which is just as well because I have no idea how that would work. With hindsight, I can see what a ridiculous thing it is to say out loud. There must be pregnant women up and down the country turning to their partners, screaming, 'YOU ARE NOT PREGNANT! I am pregnant! Do you want to know how I know I'm pregnant? No? Well, I'm telling you anyway. It's the constant nausea/swollen ankles/peanut bladder/backache/boob-ache/side-ache/ water retention and lack of sleep! So, wipe that stupid smug look off your face and make me a cup of tea!'

Announcing 'WE ARE PREGNANT' is as irritating as those people who talk about themselves in the third person.

'Gina was thrilled.'

'Who's Gina? What are you on about? Hang on, aren't you Gina ... ?'

I'm sure for some women being pregnant is great, but in my book, knowing there was going to be a baby but me not being actually pregnant was the best of every world. Seriously, what's not to like? I got to down as much red wine as I liked, stuff my face with unpasteurised cheese, shellfish and sashimi, and wash it all down with a double espresso, and all the while Chloe was growing a human inside her. It was win-win really.

Because of the IVF, our first scan was at six weeks rather than the normal twelve-week scan, which is routine when you get up the duff naturally. This early scan would hopefully confirm that Chloe was still pregnant and that all was progressing as hoped with a healthy embryo and a strong foetal heartbeat. This was when we found out the 'good' news.

I watched the sonographer squeeze on the gel and then press the ultrasound to Chloe's stomach. Gently but firmly moving it in a circular motion, her eyes focused intently on the black and white image on the screen. I also stared at the screen, anxiously squinting my eyes, trying to make out what, if anything, I was supposed to be looking at.

'There's one heartbeat ... and *there* is the OTHER heartbeat,' she said, somewhat matter-of-factly.

'Sorry ... WHAT?'

'Congratulations! You're having twins!'

I'm not sure if it's usual to scream in this situation, but that is what happened next. My mouth just opened and out it burst – an ear-piercing, high-pitched screech. I could tell you it was a scream of delight, but I think it was more the sudden-surge-of-adrenaline-coupled-with-blind-panic type of eruption.

'TWINS? Are you sure? It's TWINS?'

'Yes, positive. If you look at the screen you can clearly see two heartbeats.'

No, you can't. If you look at the screen you can clearly see eff all. Of course, I pretended I could see; we both pretended we could see.

'Oh yeah ... I can see them. Just there, right?' I bluffed.

'No, not there. There.'

She pointed at the screen.

'Ah ...'

I don't know how anyone can see anything on those ultrasounds. Maybe it's because I was hyperventilating at the time and had a limited flow of oxygen to my brain, but to me it just looked like the fuzz on an analogue telly when the aerial is up the spout.

'Look, one is here and the other is ... here!' she tried again.

'Sorry, where am I looking?'

She tried again, 'Follow my finger and you can see twin one's heart beating and if you look there, that's it's ...'

'Penis?'

'Head.'

After a while, I just nodded and made the right noises to spare myself any further embarrassment.

It might have been sensible if we had gone into that first scan with all the self-awareness of a couple that had chosen to transfer two blastocyst embryos, rather than just one. Unfortunately not. The truth is we'd had so many disappointments up until this point, all we could do prior to the scan was try to manage our expectations.

It was only after the scan when we had stared into that fuzzy screen that the reality set in. We really were going to be parents. We were going to be the parents of twins. We had the proof in the form of an ultra-sound photo ...

What the hell were we doing? How on earth were we going to cope? WOULD WE SURVIVE IT? We didn't think any of those things; not straight away. It was just so surreal and unreal and fantastical for Chlo to even *be* pregnant, it was all we could do to get our heads around that, never mind the fact that we were going to have twins. Plus, it was ages away. AGES. We had literally seven and a half months.

In the weeks after the scan we were walking on air. I was immediately obsessed with the mobile phone app that tells you what's happening to the baby in utero day by day, week by week. I scrutinised it religiously every day, roughly four times a day, to see what changes, if any, might have taken place since my last check-in.

'Oh my God, Chlo. They're about three inches long! We have two three-inch babies!'

'They're the size of a grapefruit, how big is that? Do we have any grapefruits in the fridge? Right, I'm going out to buy one!'

'They're producing URINE! They are literally piss-ing inside of you!'

'Eyebrows! They've got eyebrows now, Chloe!'

Imagine listening to *that* for nine whole months? No need, I ran out of steam after about five.

As Chloe's bump formed, then started to grow, it seemed that time actually slowed down. Those nine months felt like nine long years. Perhaps time would slow down so completely that we'd never have to move on from this naive honeymoon period where we could enjoy announcing to people 'we' were pregnant … WITH TWINS!

'Ha-ha! Look at their faces, they weren't expecting us to say that!'

'Yeah, they had no idea we'd say TWINS. Ha! What a shock for THEM!'

I've said it before, but I'll say it again, what a pair of spanners.

I'd seen people struggling with one baby, so in the back of my mind I knew having twins was going to be a challenge. In truth, however, I still hadn't given much thought to what the actual day-to-day reality would be like. At this stage, nothing in our lives had really changed except that Chlo was growing two human beings inside her and I was trying to write a new show in time for the Edinburgh Festival that August. I know, it's a big deal, writing a show can be all-consuming, let me tell you. I had no idea what it would be like once you added two babies to the mix. How could I?

One thing we had thought about, though, was where we were going to put the babies when they arrived. As soon as we found out that we were having twins, we knew we had to move house. Chlo and I were living in a one-bed flat in Archway, north London. Neither of us wanted to leave London, at least not to start with. We loved London, we still do. It had always been my home. I was born in London, went to school in south-west London and spent my entire life living in London. But we needed more space if we were going to have two children, we couldn't afford to get a bigger flat in our area and we didn't want to live in a two-bedroom flat ten miles south of zone six. We couldn't stay in London.

Chloe grew up in a village and had always wanted to live somewhere in the country, preferably by the sea.

'How about Devon?' she suggested.

'I would rather have my face dragged down a broken mirror.' I said.

'Somerset?'

'No thank you.'

'What about Dorset?'

'Absolutely not.'

I'm not dissing anyone's home county here, but I'm from London, and you can't just move a Londoner into a remote village in the middle of nowhere with no friends and questionable mobile phone reception and expect said person not to go stark staring bonkers. I like shops and houses and people and cinemas and pubs and lots and lots of different restaurants and cafes and bars and theatres and music venues. I also want my dwelling place to be diverse and multicultural, with people of all sorts of different social backgrounds, as well as a visible queer and trans community ...

I want ... well, I suppose I want somewhere like London really.

We went on day trips to market towns around London and found a hundred different reasons why we didn't want to move to any of them.

'It's way too white here.'

'It's way too posh.'

'That woman just gave me a funny look. Do you think she knows we're gay?'

'I think she knows *you're* gay ...'

As a gay couple soon to be bringing up twins, we couldn't just plant ourselves anywhere and hope that people would be OK about it. I didn't want our children to be the only ones in school with two mums. That had to be a consideration. School is hard enough without having to explain why your dad has very small wrists ... and tits.

You'd think the first place we would have thought of is the alternative, gender-queer, trans-focused, feminist-led, Pride flag-waving, green-voting, allotment-loving, organic muesli-munching vegan city that is Brighton. You'd think.

We had lots of friends there too, most of whom had campaigned tirelessly for at least five years to get us to move down. But we had other considerations, or at least Chloe did.

'We can't just move somewhere without exploring alternatives! What if we move to Brighton and then realise that we've made a mistake and wish we'd moved to St Albans?'

Yeah, that seemed really likely. (No offence, St Albans, I'm sure you are lovely.)

'I still think we should move to Brighton.'

'Let's just see what Petersfield is like before we make any big decisions ...'

Jesus wept.

Six months later we moved to Brighton.

We had bought a house. Granted, it needed a lot of work but we liked its vibe and a vibe is very important, even if that vibe is code for gutting the ENTIRE HOUSE and rebuilding it from the inside out.

With hindsight, that was a bad vibe.

We felt so smug and grown-up, what with the pregnancy and the move, but we were in la-la land about what the house refurbishment entailed. We waited months to choose a builder and because the entire place needed gutting, no sooner had we moved in than we had to move back out and pay for an Airbnb just five minutes away from the house we had bought. I don't know what we were thinking either.

I realise just how much privilege I'm choking on as I write. Oh boo-hoo! Poor us buying a house and having to do it up in one of the nicest cities in the country!

I hate me too.

We got help, OK? Yes, prudent Chlo had savings, but mainly we could afford to buy the house because our parents helped us out with the money for a deposit, and Chloe's aunt and uncle bailed us out with the rent for the Airbnb. That's what privilege is, being given stuff that frankly you don't deserve because you're stupidly lucky to have people who love you enough to help.

As soon as we moved, we knew we'd made the right decision: I don't know how or why it took us so long to realise that Brighton should have been our first and only choice from the beginning. Brighton had everything we liked about London – great coffee, shops, culture, pubs, restaurants – but with the big added bonus of the sea air, general left-leaning attitude, friendly people and lots and lots and lots of gays per square mile. We immediately felt a sense of community that we just didn't have or hadn't sought out in London.

I'm sure any town we moved to would have been perfectly tolerant of our gayness, but the fact is we didn't want to be tolerated. Like most gay people we just wanted to blend in and be accepted. When we finally became parents, we wanted our children to grow up seeing their family reflected back at them by other kids with same-sex parents.

The prospect of having twins was seismic enough without the stress of wondering if we were going to be the only gays in the village.

Now we'd done our big move and we were all settled, if only in the temporary Airbnb, we started to relax into our pregnant state of mind. Chloe had bought a couple of pregnancy and mother and baby books, and of course I was still a regular visitor to my week-by-week app. The more we read, the more it seemed that pregnancy advice consisted mainly of a list of things that pregnant women are made to feel guilty about.

Everyone has an opinion about what a pregnant woman should or shouldn't do, your friends, family, even strangers in the street: don't eat this; don't drink that; if you look at a peanut on a Tuesday afternoon while walking past a shop that sells unpasteurised cheese your baby will probably have right-wing tendencies. EVERYONE: PLEASE CHILL OUT!

My advice to Chloe was that it was her pregnancy, her body, our babies and, therefore, she should do what felt best for her. I decided that a nine-month guilt trip was the last thing either of us needed, so I proudly announced my own list.

First Rule of pregnancy: don't judge yourself.

Second Rule of pregnancy: don't judge other women.

Third Rule of pregnancy: RELAX.

So, yes, Chloe had the occasional glass of wine and I actively encouraged it – see my Brister's Rules of Pregnancy above. Also, I don't like to drink alone and I think my needs should be taken into consideration here. I'm kidding! (I'm not.)

We started nesting. Well, Chlo started nesting. I just watched her with growing alarm. I was overwhelmed by the amount of stuff you're expected to buy. It was totally ridiculous. You could spend hundreds of pounds on shit you don't really need, or could get cheaper or free somewhere else. Why would you spend £15 on one baby grow? Get a grip. The baby is going to vomit and shit on/in it for three weeks and then outgrow it! Also, what nutter is spending £500 on a high chair? What is the matter with you? You do realise it's only going to get covered in avocado and pureed sweet potato and you can get a perfectly nice one for £30 from IKEA! Jesus wept … . Sorry, I completely forgot that I am in no position to judge anyone about anything. Everyone has the right to choose whatever varnished mahogany high chair or pure cashmere baby grow they want. Please carry on.

I say that as someone who is a clueless idiot that has absolutely no currency in terms of knowing anything about anything, but it's so hard not to judge, isn't it? And while I'm at it, I just need to get one other thing off my chest: rich first-time mums who have managed to make parenthood into a competitive branding exercise can go fuck themselves. I'm sorry, love, but you can take your Boden catalogue, your trendy Bugaboo and your soya decaf flat white and shove them up your self-satisfied …

Sorry, sorry! I realise I need help with sticking to my Second Rule of pregnancy. This not judging business is harder than it looks.

Despite the very generous help from family, money was still an issue for us, plus we were preparing for the arrival of *two* babies, so almost everything we had was either donated, or bought from a second-hand shop or one of the many online mother and baby groups.

Looking at all the baby stuff we were accumulating, it was hard to imagine an actual baby fitting into one of the many baby grows we had, or lying in the Moses baskets we'd inherited. The whole idea of actual human babies existing and taking up space in our lives still seemed like a bizarre fantasy. But no one could say we weren't ready: we had the gear, the house (almost), and we were even thinking about their names!

At our twenty-week scan, we had made the decision that having twins was surprise enough: we wanted to know the sex of our children. In the back of my mind, I was still hanging on to that dream of having a daughter, and having twins meant that the odds had to be on my side. We were bound to have at least one girl, right? Wrong, we were having twin dreaming boys. I'd be lying if I said I wasn't a little disappointed, but it was only for about a minute or two, and I was quickly swept up in the excitement of imagining who these little people, my sons, were going to be.

Now, that we knew their sex, we had loads of time to come up with their names. But boy, did we take it to the wire. Anyone will know that choosing a name for your child is a big responsibility. You don't want to get it wrong and ruin your child's life. Some parents seem to forget that they are giving a name to an actual independent human being:

'We didn't want our daughter to have one of the more common top fifty names. We wanted something unique, something original that really spoke to us, which is why we called her Puree. We've always loved tomatoes and neither of us like chewing, do we, darling?'

Some couples have a name in mind right from the outset, at least for the first baby, and so it's easy. Not for me and not for Chloe. Oh no. We could not agree on a single name, mainly because Chloe has terrible taste in names. Don't roll your eyes like that, she does! OK, let me reframe that thought. Chloe has a more adventurous approach to names than I do. When it comes to children's names, I have swallowed the book of convention, baked a cake and iced 'conservative' on it and have an annual subscription to *Lady* magazine.

Depending on which room she had just walked into, Chlo randomly but consistently came up with new and ever more bizarre name choices.

'What about Coving, Jen?

'Plywood has quite a nice ring to it. Don't you think?'

'Mantlepiece is a strong name for a man.'

I had one name that I loved and my approach was to just doggedly and stubbornly offer up this name over and over again until Chloe agreed to it. I'm not saying her way wasn't any good, I'm just saying mine had a 100 per cent success rate.

So, we had one name. It was the name I wanted and I couldn't have been happier. But fair's fair, and now I had to allow Chlo the opportunity to name our second child.

'River.'

'No.'

'Indiana.'

'No.'

'Gray.'

'No.'

'Zane.'

'No.'

'Hoxton.'

'WHAT ARE YOU TALKING ABOUT?'

Look, I know some of you might be reading this and thinking, 'I LOVE ALL OF THOSE NAMES!' or 'My son is called River Indiana Gray Zane Hoxton. How dare you disparage his chosen title!' Everyone, take a chill pill. I'm just saying that I personally couldn't imagine calling one of my children any of those names.

I told you, when it comes to names, I'm a traditional kind of gal, and in my gut, I didn't connect with any of these. Another problem was other people. Everybody seemed to have an opinion and it added nothing to the experience. I'd mention a name I had decided on, and then they'd go right ahead and rain all over my parade by declaring:

'Hmmm. No. I used to know a [insert name] at school and they were a right plank.'

Or,

'That was my ex's name and they cheated on me, so if you want to name your kid after a sociopath be my guest ... '

One of my favourite responses was when I told a mate about a name I was considering. He simply said:

'I hate that name.'

Not helpful.

That was the last time I mentioned names to anyone other than Chlo. My advice to anyone who's having a baby is not to talk about it. Keep it to yourself, and announce the baby's name once it is born.

In the end we chose the second name because it was the only other name that we both liked.

'I like that one!'

'Well, let's stick it in the mix, but keep thinking about other names.'

'No, I like that one.'

'How about ... ?'

'No, I like that one.'

I don't think I need to tell you the outcome of that discussion.

In case you are thinking by now that I sound like a controlling nightmare, you need to know that I very rarely get my own way. If you don't believe me, please visit my house and take in the sights. We currently have a birdhouse hanging above a door in our living room. I did not choose that birdhouse. On more than one occasion, I have stated plainly and calmly that I really don't like the birdhouse, I never wanted the birdhouse, and thought the birdhouse looked weird. The birdhouse is still there.

5

More Up the Duff

While we farted about doing online shopping and squabbling about names, time was slowly ticking by. As the pregnancy moved inexorably forward, our lives subtly shifted into a new phase. During her second trimester, Chloe started to have difficulty breathing. If she had to walk any distance, she would frequently feel faint, or actually pass out.

One evening she collapsed at Victoria station and came to lying on the floor in the middle of the station. You'd think, in a busy public place like that, lots of people would have rushed to her aid – YOU'D THINK – but only one woman stopped to help her (I thank you, stranger lady) and that was only after she'd regained consciousness. Imagine seeing a pregnant woman lying prone on the floor of a busy London station and walking on past? WHAT IS WRONG WITH PEOPLE?

No one seemed sure of the reason for these fainting episodes. The shortness of breath, which in turn led to Chlo's feeling of faintness, could have been caused by a lack of iron or an increase in progesterone in her body. I'm no doctor, but I think the more likely reason is that she was growing two human beings in her body and her expanding uterus was pressing against her lungs. Either way, it looked like zero fun.

Into her third trimester and Chloe was big. Due to her vast size, everything had become difficult – sleeping, eating, walking, sitting, moving, breathing – and yet, unless she was in actual real pain, she rarely complained. I struggle to cope with a bout of mild hiccups if I eat my toast too quickly. Meanwhile Chloe, who was plagued by constant heartburn, wandered around the house with a bottle of Gaviscon in her hand, calmly sipping from it like it was a cold beer on a summer's day. I still can't get my head round just how Zen she was.

What was I doing during this difficult late-pregnancy time? Well, for your information, I was stepping up equally well to the challenge by disappearing to the Edinburgh Festival for an entire month.

Chloe had loyally joined me at four previous Edinburgh Festivals, where she had watched me slowly but surely fall apart, physically and emotionally. This time, she quite rightly decided to give it a miss: at eight months pregnant the last thing Chloe needed to do was schlepp up to Edinburgh only to be confronted by a neurotic partner (me) self-obsessing about why her show hadn't been reviewed by anyone and having a panic attack in the middle of the street.[1]

I'd be lying if I said I didn't obsess about my show: of course I did. Like all performers at the Festival, I was just as completely self-absorbed and lacking any perspective as ever. Like every other year, I forgot that there was an actual 'real world' outside the Fringe where no one cared if I got a four-star review in the *Scotsman*, a nomination, or indeed if a certain comedy website thought my latest offering was an affront to the world of stand-up comedy.

But, as I said, it was the best Edinburgh I'd done to date. I had something resembling an audience, for a start. That certainly helped. But the main reason was that having a pregnant partner to return home to helped me to gain a bit of perspective: the truth, I realised, was that no one, not even other comedians really, gave a toss what I was up to and we were all just navel-gazing twats who only looked up long enough to indulge in a bit of toxic schadenfreude.

[1] Correction: Three people reviewed it, one of whom was about eleven and shouldn't be allowed an opinion on anything yet!

More importantly, if anything was going to lift any dark moods I had during that month, it was the prospect of becoming a parent to twins in just over a month.

I got back to Brighton and the first thing I noticed (it was impossible not to) was how UNBELIEVABLY MASSIVE Chloe had become. Even her feet had swollen to the point she couldn't even wear Crocs[2,3,4,5] comfortably, in fact, they had started to resemble two pieces of tenderised steak.

Chlo had been pretty humongous before I left, maybe I'd forgotten just how big, but I had no idea how she was still standing in that final month of her pregnancy. Given how big her stomach was and how small her feet are, every time she stood up it seemed inconceivable that she wouldn't topple. Although, now that I think about it, since her feet were now one and a half times the width they used to be, that's probably how she was able to stay upright ...

There is no 'comfortable' when you're eight months pregnant with twins. Just trying to find a restful position to sleep came with a whole list of no-nos. After a certain number of weeks, she couldn't sleep on her

[2] Yes, Chloe wears Crocs.
[3] Yes, we've talked about it.
[4] No, I don't own a pair.
[5] Yes, I think it's weird that they suit her.

front (for obvious reasons); she shouldn't lie on her back because it can obstruct a major blood vessel (the vena cava, according to Google) that can stop blood flow to the baby. That left sleeping on her side. However, even that was limited because once you get to your third trimester the doctors encourage you to sleep on your left-hand side. Why? I DON'T KNOW! You google it this time.

I still cannot believe that pregnant women through the ages have slept in one position for three months. What do we want from pregnant women, for crying out loud? Bed sores? My advice is, just get comfortable and try and get some shut eye. You're going to need it.

Just before I left for Edinburgh, we had booked into our local NCT course. NCT – not to be confused with the popular Korean boy band of the same name, although they look lovely – is the National Childbirth Trust, the largest parent charity in the UK. Antenatal classes are just one of the services they provide and while there are lots of organisations offering these classes, NCT is the one that most people have heard of.

I'm a bit anti-organisation – I don't like being told what to do, how to do something, when to do it – and if I'm honest, I didn't really want to go to an antenatal group. Neither did Chloe, really. I hate organised anything, you know, like organised days out / package holidays / group bookings. You can't organise fun. If I'm under pressure to have organised fun, it's not fun. It's the opposite of fun, which is … well … not fun.

We'd heard all the pros and cons about NCT classes. We knew that some people feel like there's too much emphasis on women saying no to medical intervention in the groups; the controversies about how they make women feel bad if they don't want to breastfeed; and that you can be surrounded by smug bastards. But we also knew that we needed information, or reassurance, or both. We were so clueless as first-time parents we were desperate to glean any information from any source and decided that we could cherry-pick the NCT stuff we thought would work for us and ignore the rest.

If nothing else, signing up for NCT classes might help us to meet some like-minded people in the same situation as us, people who had no idea what they were doing, lived nearby and didn't mind going out for a wine or three every now and again. We were sure that an NCT group in Brighton would be awash with gays, or at least some gays, or maybe just one other gay couple who would become our BFF pregnancy buddies.

Nope, it was just us.

I felt cheated. We'd just moved to Brighton to be surrounded by homos and there wasn't a single one in our NCT group!

In the end, it wasn't that bad. Of course, there was the obligatory sit-in-a-circle-and-introduce-yourself business, which is always awful whatever the situation; but as the only 'other mother' in a group of heterosexual partners this only served to triple my awkwardness. I think this is how I introduced myself at our first NCT class, for example:

'Hello I'm Jen ... um ... I'm Chloe's partner ... we're not solicitors ... sorry, that's a joke. But ... um ... we aren't. Solicitors. We're just gay. Well, I'm gay, she's bi. Apparently, that's a thing. I'm kidding it *is* a thing! Lots of people are these days ... .'

SHUT UP, WOMAN!

The other reason why I was reluctant to join NCT classes, other than the organisation-allergy element, is that I'm not a people person. I don't like meeting new people. I'm not good at small talk or pretending to give a shit. I do stand-up comedy because I get to talk *at* people without ever having to hear what they have to say or think. If someone in the audience is stupid enough to shout something at me, I am allowed to retort with any number of horrific insults without recourse. It's almost as if the job was made for me.

Fortunately, our NCT group was a collection of people who seemed to be quite happy to admit they didn't know what the hell they're doing either. They also liked the pub. Things were looking up.

As the only same-sex couple, it did feel a bit weird to start with. Like the dads in the room, I was the not pregnant one, so I just bobbed about on the periphery trying to look and feel useful, and after the first session when no one seemed to bat an eyelid, I began to relax.

Our NCT group was run by a doula. If you don't know what a doula is, don't worry: no one does. That is, of course, unless you are a doula, you've met a doula, or you're insanely middle class and your parents called you 'Doula'. (I really hope that hasn't happened to anyone.)

Anyway, for the record, and to save you from googling it, a doula is someone who is paid to assist pregnant women before, during and after birth. They're not medically trained so they don't actually deliver the baby, but they help 'a mother' to 'relax' and prepare for labour and can also be present during the delivery to offer support and comfort. Doulas are usually women; I've never heard of a male doula, but they must exist, although, personally, I can't imagine anything more annoying than a bloke telling you what to do with your body during labour:

'You're doing really well, babe, just breathe ... don't fight your contractions, try and connect with them ...'

'Fuck off, mate, or you'll be connecting with my fist!'

That might just be me.

Our NCT doula was lovely, very non-judgemental, and gave us what I thought was a balanced viewpoint on natural births as well as what painkillers and/or interventions you could choose if the HORRIFIC pain from squeezing a human being out of a hole the size of a ten-pence piece got a bit too much.

Nothing really prepares you, however, for the experience of watching a woman 'simulate' contractions, as you sit in a circle of, at this point, acquaintances, in a community centre in the middle of the afternoon on a Sunday. As a half-Spaniard I have never felt more British in my life than I did that day, sitting in silence as I watched our doula panting and moaning for what felt like DAYS. No one dared make eye contact; we all sat mesmerised as she rolled her head back, her hands resting in her lap as she recreated each fresh wave of contractions with what can only be described as (and I don't say this lightly) wild abandon.

It wasn't that I felt embarrassed for her, quite the opposite. It was because she seemed to lack any self-consciousness that I became even more self-conscious about being part of this. There I was, a woman, in a room full of pregnant women who are about to go through one of the most seismic, life-changing experiences that any woman can go through, thinking to myself, 'What is the actual point of me being here?'

Maybe it was the surreal effect of the doula's act-ed-out-contractions performance, but I suddenly felt preposterous. I was an imposter. I know they weren't just Chloe's babies. They are our babies. I know that *now*. But at the time, as a non-pregnant woman with no biological connection to my part-ner's babies, it was hard not to feel like a third wheel at the antenatal class, and to stop myself becoming irrational and paranoid.

What if, after they rocked up, I didn't like them? That's a 'thing' right? People not liking babies? Or what if they didn't like me? To be honest, that seemed much more likely: after all, lots of people don't.

I didn't know if other non-bio parents went through the same thing, or if this was just me falling head first into a neurotic wormhole of my own making. Either way, I never voiced any of my hang-ups to anyone during our NCT sessions. You'll be pleased to hear that I had enough self-awareness to know better.

'Hi, I know that every other woman here in our circle is preparing to squeeze a human being out of a hole that, let's face it, is smaller than anyone would like, or have their stomach cut open and their baby yanked out of their womb, but could I just say that I'm feeling a bit insecure about my role as a non-biological parent. Is this a bad time?'

Instead, I internalised my emotions and got on with the job of pretending to be entirely confident in my role as 'hand holder' extraordinaire.

What I picked up from NCT was the message that pregnant women can take charge of their own bodies, they have agency and control of how their pregnancy and labour goes and, whenever possible, women should be encouraged to have a natural birth. Which in theory is great.

In theory.

There was a lot of emphasis on the importance of writing your birth plan (print multiple copies to be handed to everyone and anyone when you go into labour), the benefits of listening to meditation CDs, the imperative to massage your perineum. We listened religiously, took copious notes, went home and did our homework.

I'd never heard a meditation CD before, but when Chloe asked me to listen to hers, I'd never felt so tense in my life:

'Why is she heavy-breathing?'

'Who?'

'The woman on this bloody CD?'

'She's helping me to focus on my breathing.'

'Is it helping?

'Not really, I keep falling asleep …'

'How can you sleep with this woman droning on? Chlo … CHLO!'

Which brings us on to perineal massage. The perineum is the area between your bum and your genitals, and during childbirth – well, there's no nice way of putting it – this area can tear. I know: not something to be thinking about when you're eating jam on toast … I'll eat it later.

Pregnant women are advised to massage oil on to the area so that it's less likely to tear during labour. I thought that sounded like quite a nice recommendation that I could be involved with and even slightly erotic. Except That Isn't What It Is At All.

The truth is perineal massage isn't an actual massage; what you're actually doing is sticking two thumbs into your partner's vajayjay, pulling down and *stretching* her perineum. I'm not sure I nailed the technique:

'Ow! What are you doing?'

'I haven't done anything yet, I'm just trying to stick a thumb in.'

'Can you please be a bit more gentle?'

'I don't know how to stick my thumb in gently! Maybe we should lube the area first …'

'Yes, please do …'

'OK, how about this?'

'FUCK ME! What are you doing now?'

'I've got two thumbs in!'

'Well, get them out! GET THEM OUT!'

Less of a massage and more of a 'moment' that we don't speak of.

We kept up with our NCT classes and kept with the programme, doing most of the stuff they told us to do, just because it helped Chlo and me feel like we were moving forward. It gave us the illusion of control.

We wrote a birth plan. We were encouraged to visualise the birth we wanted (an easy one). We then discussed our birth plans in our circle. Everyone agreed that a natural birth was best (none of us had a clue), preferably in a warm birthing pool, listening to whale music. Significant others would be at the ready with a cool damp cloth to mop the labouring partner's brow as they used all the breathing techniques that they had learned from their meditation CDs (if you bothered to listen to it) to push out their baby with little to no drama into the waiting arms of their loving partner.[6]

There was so much emphasis on having a non-interventionist and natural birth that if, for any number of reasons, you didn't get to have that, I worried it would make the pregnant women feel like they had somehow failed. As a woman and the 'other one', I could see how this pressure could negatively impact on Chloe.

---

[6] Yeah, that didn't happen. The dream birth plan of water births, meditation CDs and medical-free deliveries was not on the cards for anyone. Every single woman in our NCT group had some kind of intervention during labour.

Whatever anyone says, whatever our plans for a natural, pain-free birth to the soaring sounds of the humpbacks, childbirth isn't always straightforward. Any number of factors or unexpected circumstances can mean that medical intervention is necessary. That doesn't make these 'unusual' or 'unnatural' births; frankly, if a woman successfully gives birth to a healthy baby and no one dies in the process, that should be a big enough cause for celebration. You're alive, your baby's alive! WELL DONE!

As I say, as the 'other one' I felt more immune to the pressures of it all. I didn't feel held up to particular standards like the expectant mums. Equally, I didn't feel that I couldn't hold my own opinion, as some of the dads admitted to me. In many ways, when you don't fit into the mum or dad column, you get to go ahead and make your own roles and rules: I was in a unique position to consider my role as a parent outside gender expectation.

At one of our many hospital appointments (you see a lot more doctors when you have twins), we were told that the chances of Chloe giving birth naturally were pretty slim. Both twins were breech, which meant they were sitting feet first in the womb, and under those circumstances an elective caesarean was on the cards. Naturally, we were devastated (*in no way whatsoever!*) but on the plus side the meditation CD was back in its case.

At this stage, it became clear to me quite quickly that most doctors genuinely couldn't give a rat's bum if you have a natural birth or not. They just want everyone to walk out of the hospital alive. Our doctor told us that a fixed date for the operation would be booked in less than two weeks. In the meantime, did we have any questions about having twins? Questions? Hmmm, let me see … You might think that our response was, 'HOW LONG HAVE YOU GOT, MATE?'

Instead we just shook our heads politely:

'No, I don't think we have any questions … Do you, love?'

'Erm … no. I think we know what we're doing.'

Know what we're doing? Do me a bloody favour. We had no idea.

With just a fortnight to go before the caesarean date, Chlo and I decided that we were going to make the most of our last weeks alone together before the birth. Because that's what people do, right? They ignore the fact that their lives are about to irrevocably change until the final fortnight, then they panic and start making restaurant reservations.

I booked for lunch at a popular French restaurant in Brighton. We sat down and naturally I ordered myself a glass of red wine.

'I think I'd like a glass too,' said Chloe.

'Oh … Well, you should have one. The only thing is you look REALLY pregnant.'

'Do you think the waiter would judge me?'

'I dunno, it's just the pregnant thing ...'

'You're right. I'll just have a mineral water.'

'*Bonjour*, may I take your order?'

'Yes, um ... I would like a glass of the Pinot Noir ...'

'How about a carafe for you both to share?'

The French don't give a shit. Here's a tip: if you ever do want a drink when you are pregnant, I can highly recommend going to a French restaurant.

Or, better still, just move to Bordeaux. I liked the French approach to pregnancy. Of course, you want to keep your unborn baby healthy and safe. On the other hand, if you fancy the occasional glass of wine or a slice of brie, you shouldn't be taken out onto the street to be publicly flagellated. As I have said, and I will say it again: remember Brister's Rules and RELAX. It's your pregnancy, your body, your baby and you should do what feels best for you.

I look back at those pre-babies days in Brighton with rose-tinted spectacles. I confess that I am usually about as romantic as a breeze block, but I couldn't have been more in love with Chlo than I was during that time. Don't get me wrong, we're still in love (I think, it's hard to tell sometimes) but during those final few weeks we really connected and our relationship felt rock solid. We were so excited about the prospect of becoming parents.

Imagine the scene. We walked arm in arm through a rosy mist on our daily evening stroll along Brighton seafront. We soaked up the view, and talked hopefully and excitedly about our future together with our brand-new family.

Ah, it's so rosy. So very rosy. The day before Chloe's caesarean every routine action was done with the weight of knowing it would be the last time we did it before the twins were born.

'This is my last shower before we're parents!'

'This is the last load of washing I'll do before we're parents!'

'This is the last cream cracker I'll eat before we're parents!'

'This is the last time we ...'

'YES, I GET IT, JEN!'

That evening we had decided to go on a date to the cinema to see *Pride* and in true Chloe/Jen fashion we went with two mates. We know how to do romance. With hindsight, I think our friends may have been more excited than we were.

'CAN YOU BELIEVE YOU'RE GONNA BE PARENTS?'

'THIS TIME TOMORROW YOU'LL HAVE TWINS!'

'OH. MY. GOOOOOOOOOD!'

'AAAAAAAAARGGGGGH!'

I think it's the most excited any four people have ever been in the multistorey car park at Brighton Marina.

That night we lay in bed holding hands, staring into each other's eyes, wide-eyed and apprehensive.

By 9.30am the very next morning we would be parents.

6

Ninety-Six Hours on
Maternity Ward Three

On the morning of the caesarean I woke up feeling giddy with excitement. I say excitement, it was almost certainly adrenaline. If I'd had to, I think I could have run a marathon that morning (OK, maybe 5k then, at least).

With an elective caesarean, most of the decisions were taken for us. We just did what we were told. On the one hand, this gave us a sense of security; on the other hand, it made us feel like the entire experience of childbirth was out of our control.

The one thing I had done that definitely made me feel useful was that I had made a playlist on a CD of our favourite music for the birth. If that wasn't a good use of my time I don't know what is. I very carefully chose tracks that we both liked, while also ignoring any music that Chloe really wanted.

'We are not having Pearl Jam on the playlist.'

'I'm the one giving birth and I want Pearl Jam.'

'I do not want to listen to "Even Flow" during the birth of our children!'

'Well, then you can't have three songs by James Vincent McMorrow!'

'That's not fair, you've got George Michael and Tracy Chapman!'

'YOU LOVE TRACY CHAPMAN!'

'FOR THE SAKE OF THIS ARGUMENT I'M GOING TO PRETEND I DON'T!'

It was a great bonding exercise and we felt all the closer for doing it.

We had to be at the hospital for 7.30am so that Chlo could be prepared for her caesarean, which was scheduled for 9.30am. I'll be honest with you, most of that day is a blur. The main side effect of adrenaline for me is almost certainly memory loss, although happily, I had remembered to pack the CD.

I also remember that we were met on the ward by our two midwives, who introduced themselves and reassured us that everything was going to be fine. They settled us in, and showed Chloe how to put on a theatre gown. They handed me some scrubs. They told us to give them a shout if we wanted anything. Did we have any questions? Did we need anything?

What did we need? I had no idea, maybe someone could hold my hand? I was so nervous. I don't think I'd ever been more nervous in my life. Every emotion felt heightened. I felt elated (we were about to become parents!). Terrified (what if something went wrong?). And overwhelmed (for the love of God, don't start crying before we even get into the operating room).

By this point Chloe was dressed in her blue backless hospital gown and getting ready to be wheeled in for the BIG OPERATION!

Is there any situation more surreal than the one where you walk into a room with the full knowledge that in less than an hour you're going to walk out as the parents of TWINS?

The answer is, no there isn't. And I don't want to argue about it, OK?

When a woman gives birth to twins, we discovered, you get double everything. We'd already met the two midwives. We also had two obstetricians, two nurses and an anaesthetist, plus two other people who were also doctors who came in and out. To this day I have no idea what their role was. Suffice to say, it was crowded in there. It was starting to feel less intimate by the minute, but I had my masterstroke at the ready:

'Can we put this CD on?'

'Yeah, that's no problem ... Hmmm, actually, I don't think the CD's working.'

'It should work. I played it before we got here ...'

'I don't think it's the CD. I think this player is broken. Do you still want music?'

'Umm ... Ideally ...'

'DOES ANYONE KNOW IF WE HAVE ANOTHER CD PLAYER THAT WORKS?'

'I THINK THERE'S ONE NEXT DOOR!'

'CAN YOU GRAB IT FOR ME!'

'YEAH, SURE. DO YOU NEED THE ADAPTOR?'

'NO, WE'RE FINE!'

You see? A masterstroke. Much more intimate and relaxing.

We did get a CD player and it played the music we wanted and even at the level we wanted it. Meanwhile Chlo had been given the necessary drugs for the operation and was, to put it bluntly, off her face.

I was taking the responsibility of our birth plan very seriously: I wasn't just given the task of playing music, oh no! I had far bigger fish to fry.

We had both listened to enough episodes of BBC *Woman's Hour* and spent enough time on the internet to know the pluses and minuses of caesarean births. One of the most common concerns was that babies can be born with fluid in their lungs. They can also be distressed from being pulled out so quickly and dramatically from the womb, not to mention all the stuff about their immune system.

Chlo had embarked on some extensive research (Google) and read that babies born by caesarean also have a greater chance of contracting allergies later in life. This is because they aren't being pushed through the birth canal and picking up their mother's vaginal microbes on the way out, which, it's believed, can help boost a baby's immune system.

Honestly, though, if you spend enough time on the internet you will convince yourself that the moon landing never happened and that contraception is a feminist conspiracy started by lesbian lizards who want to castrate all men and continue the human race by growing yeast in a petri dish and mixing it with fairy liquid. This may or may not be true but even so, it's really not the best place to make rational decisions.

But, after discovering this birth-canal-microbe-baby-allergy business, it hadn't taken us long to start reading about vaginal seeding. Let me explain. Basic-ally, the newborn baby has their face and mouth swabbed with their mother's vaginal fluid to mimic the natural transfer of these microbes during vaginal delivery. With one caveat: you can't really replicate the process after the fact, and you can't know if they are the same microbes the baby would be exposed to naturally during a vaginal labour, or if you're just rubbing your baby's snout in tons of potentially harmful bacteria.

Should we or should we not go for a vaginal seeding once our babies were delivered? Let's just say that at the time, we thought it sounded like a reasonable question to put to a doctor. After all, it seemed (according to Google) that there were people in the medical profession using this practice and plenty of mothers were advocating it as a means of augmenting their baby's immune system.

I spoke to one of the midwives. She said we should go for it, but that we had to consult the obstetricians:

'Sorry ... I know you're busy and I don't want to interrupt ... but do you think we could swab the babies with vaginal fluid when they're born?'

'What?'

'It's a thing to help with the baby's immune ...'

'You want to what? What is she talking about?'

'We just read that ...'

'I'm not doing that. Why would anyone want to swab a newborn baby in vaginal fluid? I'm sorry but that's ridiculous ...'

That was a 'No' then.

Meanwhile, Chloe was high as a kite on the anaesthetic and completely unaware that any of this was going on. I don't think I'd ever seen her more relaxed about any situation; in fact, I had seen her a lot more stressed trying to open a jam jar than when she was lying there about to have our twins.

'This is lovely, I'm having such a nice time. Are you having a good time, Jen?'

'Never better ... My knees are sweating, though. Is that normal?'

A curtain had been placed to separate the top half of Chloe, where I was sitting, and her bottom half, where all the action was happening. I really wanted to see what was going on, plus I had promised Chloe that I'd film it. (Yes, you're reading this correctly, Chloe wanted me to film having her children pulled out of an open wound in her stomach. And yes, I did think that was a great idea.)

However, the doctors had made it clear that in order to keep the area sterile I needed to stay where I was. Our midwife (let's call her Jane) knew that we wanted to do a video and had a plan.

'OK, when the baby comes out, I'm going to give you a signal and then you can stand up and film or take photos.'

Perfect! That was the plan.

That moment when the first of our twins was pulled out of Chloe's womb is etched forever in my memory.

'Looks like Twin Two has turned so we're going to get him out first, OK?'

Did I answer? I can't remember. At this point I had so much adrenaline pumping through my body I thought I was going to explode.

Jane gave me the signal, her eyes widening, she mouthed: 'NOW!' I looked back at her, frozen to my seat. I couldn't stand up and the moment was gone. In the hands of the doctor was a baby. He was crying loudly, blue and pink and covered in a yellowish scum, the thick veiny umbilical cord still attached to his tiny body.

'That's the first one out.'

There was no time to take in the fact that one of our sons had been born before the second one was ready to be delivered. I heard Jane say:

'Now!'

With my camera in hand, I quickly stood up and watched as our second son was pulled from the warmth and safety of Chloe's womb and into the cold, harsh lights of the hospital room. I had caught it all on camera! RESULT.

Meanwhile, tiny Twin Two had been towelled and was ready to be weighed.

'Would you like to cut the cord?' a midwife asked me, holding the little bundle in her arms.

I knew that I would have to cut the cord. I had been looking forward to it as a momentous occasion in the birth of our sons. Now, faced with this bloody, veiny rope, I felt less inclined.

'Take the scissors, you'll find it's quite tough.'

It was tough, like trying to cut through an electric cable.

'Quickly! We need to get him warm.'

I cut through the cord and watched as it bled! It was fine. No one said anything, so that must be normal. I was standing around like a fart in the wind. I noticed that Twin One had been placed on Chloe's chest who really did look like she was on the best Class As of her life.

I turned back.

'Would you like to hold your son?'

'My son?'

I was handed Twin Two, this tiny bundle, and immediately I lifted the front of my blue scrubs for the obligatory skin-to-skin contact.

I hold our newborn son under my scrubs. He is so small, but in that moment, I don't even notice. I feel his heartbeat slow down as it falls into sync with mine. I am completely overwhelmed and I appear to be crying like the walking cliché that is a new parent. I don't care. I'd been wanting to cry for the last hour.

It was 9.30-something-am on 25 September 2014 and Chloe and I were suddenly the parents to twin boys.

This entire day is a blur to me in so many ways, but I know we were moved to a different room. I remember that Chloe was smiling, she looked ridiculously happy – I'm not sure if this was the drugs, the hormones or a heady cocktail of both. I was relieved that she didn't appear to be the slightest bit overwhelmed. Our sons were placed on her chest, and they seemed to know exactly what to do. Within minutes of giving birth, she was breastfeeding our boys. I was in awe!

How come everyone knew what they were doing apart from me?

Because we had twins, but also because they were both pretty small, the midwife team were keeping a close eye on the babies' progress. Twin Two was not feeding as well and not putting on enough weight, so we were kept in an extra couple of days so they could monitor him.

I wasn't going anywhere, but the ward had run out of the mattresses for partners, so I slept on a camp bed. I could have slept on anything because I really didn't get much sleep anyway. The babies were awake every hour, and I was either changing nappies, lifting them so Chlo could feed them, or moving them back into their cot. The adrenaline pumping through my veins was enough to keep me going.

In the end, we spent four days and four nights in the hospital, for which I will FOREVER be grateful.[1] Twin One was 5 pounds 11 ounces and Twin Two was 4 pounds 5 ounces: you could lift and cradle them in the palm of one hand. Not a single one of the baby grows we had packed fit our boys. Even the tiniest newborn ones were two sizes too big.

---

[1] Really and truly the NHS is a wondrous and marvellous institution that we all take for granted in this country. Try having a caesarean in the US without insurance and it'll cost you over fifty grand. But, hey, let's not concern ourselves with the fact that it's being sold off bit by bit right from under our feet.

During the time we spent in hospital we were very well looked after, but the differing advice from one nurse to another at times felt bewildering.

'Why have you covered the babies in blankets? They're going to get far too hot!'

'You need to ensure your babies are kept warm, remember they're used to being in the womb.'

'Make sure you wake them up to feed them, they must be fed every couple of hours.'

'Don't wake them, they'll wake up naturally. Just feed them a bit longer when they're up, it's important for you to rest too.'

We didn't know whether we were coming or going at times.

'Guys, could I perhaps suggest that you have a mid-wife meeting, decide on what exactly it is that we're supposed to be doing and then get back to us?'

Of course, babies aren't a one-size-fits-all, but it would have been nice not to have conflicting advice thrown at us every twelve hours, and then admonished and made to feel like idiots for seemingly getting it wrong, even though we were just doing exactly what the midwife on the last shift had told us to do.

Chloe was becoming upset and emotional (two things I didn't recognise in her) because Twin Two was not putting on weight and was not feeding as well as his brother. I hadn't ever really seen Chloe upset

before, not like this. There was a feeling of panic coming from her that worried me.

The little chap cried a lot more than his brother and
only seemed comfortable lying on his front, which we
were told we should not allow under any circumstances because of the risk of cot death. He hated
being on his back and as soon as we placed him on his
front, he stopped crying and would go straight to sleep.

So, guess what, we put him on his front.

Does this make us bad parents? No, it doesn't.

Does this mean we both kept waking him up to
check he was breathing? Yes, it does.

We were told to feed him extra to top up his breastfeeding. Chloe expressed colostrum (the stuff mums
produce for newborns, before it becomes milk) and we
tried to feed it to him using a syringe. He wasn't having it. Why would he? He was getting the exact same
stuff from a soft warm nipple. Why on earth would he
want a plastic syringe stuffed into his mouth?

But we could tell that he was hungry and it was
hardly surprising. The doctor explained that the pla-
centa that had been feeding him was half the size of
his brother's and had all but stopped nourishing him in
the womb, hence his lower birth weight.

For the first three nights I seemed to manage OK
with no sleep, but on the fourth night on the ward,
I finally crashed. I felt delirious, my whole life felt
dream-like and out of control. All I could think about

was getting some shut-eye. Sleep seemed like the greatest and most luxurious thing I could indulge in.

Chloe, who had had about as much sleep as me, bizarrely, had never looked better:

'Are you tired?' I asked her.

'A little bit.'

'A little bit? I feel like this conversation is some kind of dream sequence.'

'You've always needed more sleep than me.' Chloe said.

(This is categorically not true. I'm sure every comedian gets this levelled at them, but the truth is we work NIGHTS so we get home LATE which is why we need to sleep in a bit in the morning.)

'Sometimes I stay up late and we go to bed at the same time and you still sleep for hours longer than me in the morning.' She must have been reading my mind.

'True, but let's not forget I have often driven or been on a train for hours as well as working, which is tiring.'

'You're only on stage for twenty minutes, so it's not really "work", is it?'

'IT IS WORK! IT IS! I'M SORRY BUT IT JUST IS!'

'Not proper work like a nurse, or a doctor, or a teacher or a social worker, or a PA in an office or a plumber or a ...'

'Yes, yes, I get it. I don't have a proper job. I'm still tired, OK?' I wasn't in the mood for this conversation right then, right there, so I huffily manoeuvred myself on my thin camp bed, turned my back to Chloe, and pretended to go to sleep.

I wasn't tired, though, not really. I had no idea what tired was. Tired was still to come.

Fortunately, by the fourth day it seemed like some of the extra feeding was getting in because the little one started to put on weight. The doctors told us we could take our babies home and Chloe returned to her usual even self.

On the day we were to leave, a nurse we had never met before cheerily walked in and saw me lounging on my little camp bed.

'Why are you sleeping on a camp bed? We've got mattresses you can sleep on,' she said.

'I was told you'd run out of mattresses.'

'No, we haven't. We've got a room full of them.'

It's fine, I've let that go, in fact I loved sleeping on a camp bed the exact width of my body. It was a dream.

The day we left the hospital I felt more than a little highly strung. I had gone home to collect the car so we could drive us all home. It didn't feel right that we should be leaving with these two tiny boys on our own. Surely someone should come home with us? Make sure we know what we're doing? Offer us round-the-clock advice should we need it? They can't seriously expect us to look after two newborn babies with no assistance whatsoever?

But, not only did they let us leave unaccompanied, they practically escorted us off the ward.

'Lovely to have you, blah blah blah BYE-EEEE!'

Whoosh, and the ward doors closed behind us.

We had our two tiny bundles strapped in their car seats, in their oversized 'tiny baby' baby grows they looked like two little dolls. It was only when we got outside that the sheer terror of what was ahead of us hit me.

These two baby boys were 'ours'. We were solely responsible for them, no one else. Up until this point, I had only been responsible for myself and even then, if things really hit the skids, Mum would intervene.

Putting these two most precious things in a car suddenly seemed like madness:

'Have you strapped them in?'

'Yes, they're both strapped in.'

'Can you just double-check?'

'I'm in the back of the car now, so I can see they're strapped in.'

'So, just check again ...'

'I am checking.'

'And?'

'They're still strapped in!'

The drive from the hospital to our house was fifteen minutes maximum, less than that with no traffic. It had gone 9pm so there wasn't much traffic on the road, but I navigated the car as carefully as I could out of the hospital car park and onto the main road. I was hyper-vigilant, wary of every car and every pedestrian, but whatever I did, it wasn't quite careful enough.

'You're going too fast.'

'I'm doing less than twenty miles an hour.'

'Well, that's too fast. Slow down.'

'If I go any slower, we won't be moving!'

'What are you doing?'

'I have to turn right here …'

'Can you try and turn right without quite so much movement?'

It was a longer journey than either of us anticipated.

7

Connect Four

Our first weeks back at home, or our second home in the Airbnb, as a brand-new family were intense and anxious, but also so wonderful, in so many ways.

Chlo was astonishing: an absolute machine. She was breastfeeding both babies, getting little to no sleep and yet she still managed to project-manage the house renovation, which was ongoing.

From the ease with which she held the baby boys and the way they immediately relaxed when they were resting on her chest or in her arms, it was plain to see that Chloe was a natural at motherhood. She had clearly bonded with the babies from day one. Her smell, her voice, her milk was all they wanted. I, on the other hand, was an alien to them, or at least that's how it felt to me.

That bond that a mother and baby may instinctively and intuitively have doesn't always happen for a biological birth mother either, for any number of reasons, whether it be postnatal depression or just the overwhelming exhaustion and pressure of looking after a baby.

The same goes for breastfeeding, most women want to do it but sometimes your baby doesn't latch, maybe she has tongue tie, maybe your baby is premature so you can't breastfeed him, maybe your milk ducts are blocked, maybe breastfeeding causes you such acute pain that you can't keep doing it. Whatever the reason, I'm going to tell you to remember two very important things:

1. Don't worry about it.
2. Don't feel guilty about it.[1]

Guess what?

You don't have to breastfeed your baby because there is this great stuff called formula and formula is amazing and will feed your baby and your baby will grow and be happy and healthy and for crying out loud, it's FINE!

The most important thing to remember is that you are _feeding_ your baby. That's it. THE END.

---

[1] There, that feels better already, right?

No one has ever said, 'OK, so Dave, we think you're great, the team thinks you'd be a perfect addition, you have a proven track record in this field and frankly, your CV is second to none. But it does say here that you weren't breastfed as a baby… so… I'm sorry, it's a "no" from us.'

Never happened.

With hindsight, I can see that we were both very lucky that breastfeeding and new motherhood seemed to come so quickly and naturally to Chloe.

I was full to the brim with all kinds of feelings and emotions, but as we settled into our new reality back at home, I realised very quickly that, right now, as far as our sons were concerned, I was completely surplus to requirements.

Don't get me wrong: I was of use *practically*, of course, to everyone. I was vital to the smooth running of the whole day-to-day operation, but the babies did not need me. Their main and immediate requirement, put simply, were Chloe's breasts. I couldn't fill in where that was concerned. I could soothe them, to a point, but my smell wasn't familiar to them in the way that Chloe's was. She had grown them inside her for nine months for heaven's sake! To all intents and purposes, to the boys, I was a stranger with two point-less boobs.

I didn't feel any sadness or upset about this, it was what I was expecting. I suppose I'd hoped there'd be a little corner of need that I could squeeze myself into, which didn't involve:

'Could you get me a glass of water?'

'Hold him while I sit up.'

'I think you need to change his nappy.'

I was happy to do all of this. I wanted to be involved in any way I could.

When we told my younger brother Greg that Chloe was pregnant, I remember him saying:

'Don't worry if you don't feel anything for the first few months. It's normal. You'll fall in love with them later.'

I remember thinking it was a weird thing to say to me. *Of course* I was going to feel something. You don't not feel anything when your children are born! What did he know anyway? He was just a bloke and blokes look at things differently to women. Plus, he's my brother and therefore he was almost certainly wrong.

He wasn't wrong, but he wasn't completely right either.

I did feel something. I felt a whole smorgasbord of emotions: love, protectiveness, fear, anxiety, joy, and more love ... But, as the 'other' parent, there simply wasn't the same automatic and instinctive 'oneness' that Chloe and the boys had from the get-go. I think I just had it in my mind that I would instantly share that same connection with our boys that Chloe had formed so intuitively. I didn't. How could I?

I don't think that had anything to do with not having any 'biological' role in our babies' conception and birth. Forget biology. Once your child is born, biology means nothing, at least it did to me. Those two boys were not just Chloe's or mine they were *ours*. Even so, I was carrying around a fair bit of neurosis about connecting with them. My biggest fear, however, was what if they didn't connect with me?

Right then those two tiny blobs were strangers and I was going to have to make every effort to get to know them and for them to get to know me.

The babies were not the only thing I had to get my head around. There was also the adjustment of having my partner suddenly and intensely plunged into her new world of motherhood in which I, as the 'other' parent, existed only on her periphery. Of course, that's how it should be – I knew that Chloe had to give all of her energy and love to our two baby boys, there was no way that she could prioritise me in the same way that she had before.

It was up to me to navigate my own way between my partner and our children. I needed to find a role in this new family shape that worked for me and one that I could feel secure in.

I made a conscious choice from the get-go. I knew that, besides my relationship with Chloe, the most important thing in the world was to form a bond with my children. Whatever the reason, I committed to being as big a part of my children's lives as I could.

If that connection wasn't there instantly, I was going to bloody well dig deep and make it happen.

I knew that I wanted, or I should say, I *needed* to be 100 per cent involved; being the one responsible for the more manual side of caring for our boys gave me a purpose. The fact that Chlo couldn't get up easily because of her caesarean and because we had two babies to care for meant that I was needed. And I really needed to be needed. Not in a needy way. Well, actually, maybe in a needy way.

In fact, had I not been needed and required to do so much, I'm not sure I would have coped. I think I would have found that tough.

All of this making myself indispensable was made easier because of my job. I adapted my work schedule to fit in and give me the maximum time with Chloe and the boys. I was lucky: as a stand-up comedian I could choose to work only at weekends, or only take the work mid-week that allowed me to drive back the same night. I gave up the late nights and post-gig booze-ups for the time being. Instead I headed straight to the car park / train station the minute I left the stage. And I did it happily, knowing that soon I'd be home in Brighton with Chlo and our babies. I was happy to give up everything in return for the privilege of being a parent. Willingly and with gusto![2]

[2] Yeah, I'm saying 'gusto' with no irony. Deal with it.

... Well, I'd be lying if I said I kept up the gusto every waking moment. When that included BEING AWAKE for twenty-one hours a day.

Maybe because I'm a woman, even though I didn't actually carry and give birth to the boys, I have the same instincts as a mother that Chloe does with the boys. Even when all went quiet, I didn't relax. If, suddenly, I couldn't hear them stir, it sent me into anxious overdrive. I got up to stand over their cot every other hour to check if they were still breathing, when, let's face it, what I should have been doing was grabbing that rare moment of silence for sleep.

'I can't hear his breath.'

'He's fine, he's asleep.'

'I'm just going to check ...'

'Jen, honestly leave him ...'

'Waaaaaaaaaaaaaaahhhhhhh!'

'Yeah, you were right. He was asleep.'

Look, if it wasn't me doing it, it was Chloe. Our worst-case scenario played out in our heads over and over again as we took it in turns to wake the boys up in a frantic panic.

For the first three months, I was the one up on my feet every forty-five minutes, every single night, checking if they were warm enough, or too warm, changing nappies, lifting the boys from their Moses baskets to Chloe and back again. And I did all those night shifts with no uppers. Oh no. My body wasn't producing any happy hormones and once the adrenaline had drained, I was just a husk of a woman staggering about in the night fantasising about being in a self-induced coma because at least then I could stop lying awake listening to the babies breathing, or being jolted awake by their screams, and get some shut-eye.

Being a bit beige, I never look great in the winter; I have a hint of jaundice in my skin and I look tired even if I'm not. Now, I was beginning to resemble an extra from *The Walking Dead*. The dark circles around my eyes grew starkly pronounced and my eyes started to shrink. Turns out that's a thing. Small eyes. I had tiny eyes for about two years. I've got the photos to prove it. I'll lend you a magnifying glass and I challenge you to find my eyes in those pictures.

Chloe meanwhile had never looked better. I mean it. Even with the lack of sleep and the double breast-feeding, the woman looked incredible.

She had looked fantastic ever since the birth. Her hair, which is the thickest hair I have ever come across, was now like a mane. Lustrous, full; it hardly needed washing. Her skin was clear and her eyes had definitely not shrunk, if anything they sparkled. Chloe was having the time of her life. She'll deny this now, but let me tell you she was. On top of all of this, the pregnancy weight was falling off her; it didn't seem to matter how much she ate, or what her calorie intake was, she kept losing the pounds.

Without doubt, Chloe's rapidly diminishing bulk was largely due to the fact that the babies fed almost constantly. If you're thinking that double breastfeeding sounds horrific, I can tell you, having seen it up close, it's not great. Chloe loved everything about it. She was a bloody natural. She happily sat in bed or on the sofa with one or both of the babies, surrounded by a pile of cushions or with the double breastfeeding pillow, and the boys would feed, and feed, and feed. As she began to lose more and more weight, she positively proselytised the joys of breastfeeding the boys:

'I don't want it to end. I'm losing SO MUCH WEIGHT!'

'Remember it's not forever, if you carry on eating like you are and you stop breastfeeding ...'

'Why would I stop breastfeeding?'

'Well, because it would be weird to breastfeed an eight-year-old.'

'Maybe I could be a wet nurse?'

You think I'm making this up? I'm not, Chloe genuinely started to think of breastfeeding as a legitimate weight-loss-inducing career plan.

Meanwhile my breasts were still very much my own.

Or so you'd think. Apparently, the very fact of *having* breasts meant that I should have been thinking about putting them to use. I was at a party, chatting idly to a woman I barely knew, when the conversation took an odd turn:

'Are you going to breastfeed your children?'

'Well, no. I'm not the biological mum ... '

'You know you can breastfeed them as well?'

' ... What?'

'You do it by pumping your breasts for six to eight weeks before your baby is born. You can actually trick your body into thinking it needs to lactate.'

'WHAT THE FLICKETY FUCK ARE YOU TALKING ABOUT?'

Why on God's green earth would I want to pump my tits for two months non-stop in order to produce milk that my girlfriend produced naturally? I get that it's handy to have four boobs offering milk on tap instead of two, but who in their right mind is going to pump their tits? Have you ever stuck a pump to a non-lactating nipple? I did, for a laugh. Just to see what would happen. IT WAS AGONY. Never mind the time one of my sons managed to latch onto one of my exposed nipples when I was holding him after I got out of the shower. The pain was so acute I almost threw him off me onto the bed. I could not fathom choosing to put myself through that torture three or four times a day for two whole months.

Anyway, as far as I was concerned, it was a non-starter. I'm not convinced it would even have worked and even if it had, I was not prepared to have nipples like swollen cow teats in order to find out.

People said stupid things to me all the time. In the moment I just sort of nodded my head and smiled blankly at them, in the hope that they would stop talking. All the while my brain was screaming:

'PLEASE JUST GO AWAY!'

I think some women felt genuinely sad for me: sad that I wouldn't be able to breastfeed my children, that I wouldn't be able to experience pregnancy, that I wouldn't see my own DNA reflected and continued with the birth of my children. I knew different and didn't allow their projected feelings a second's thought.

After those early days of needy panic and neurosis, the fact is that I had somehow found my own groove between Chloe and our newborn babies. I can't remember if it took a few weeks or a few months, but the rhythm and the connection I had longed for found itself. Perhaps the relentlessness of being a new parent knocked the insecurity out of me and it simply became a matter of survival. If I threatened to indulge in any heavy-duty self-absorption, the boys intervened to give me a timely kick up the backside; such is the beauty of babies. If anything was going to force me to live in the present, it was them.

Outside of Chloe and the boys I had no care. If they were OK, I was OK. If they were happy, I was happy. If they weren't sleeping … you get the idea. There was no yesterday, or tomorrow, let alone next week. Every day revolved entirely around two small babies.

I didn't have a single anxiety dream. I was so dead to the world that I didn't dream at all. I had the ability to fall asleep as soon as my head hit the pillow and then, until my next awakening, to all intents and purposes I was unconscious.

That state, however, was a sweet, but oh so very rare treat. As the other mother, I may have been able to swerve breastfeeding, but I wasn't able to swerve the biggest challenge of all. No bloody sleep.

8

To Sleep, Perchance?

I am tired.

So very tired.

I have lost all sense of who I am, what I am doing, and what it was like to have peripheral vision. The word 'tired' does not properly encapsulate the extent of my exhaustion. I am weary, dog-tired, prostrate, exhausted, spent, sapped, drained, played out, dead beat, shattered, knackered, bushed, whacked, fagged out.

I think about sleep most of the time, all of my fantasies revolve around different places where I could rest my head for forty winks. If I see anyone asleep, whether it be someone on television, a baby in a pram or someone nodding off on a park bench, I am immediately transported to potent fantasies of my own bed. What I'm saying is, at this point in my life, my biggest ambition is being Lenny Henry in that bloody Premier Inn ad.

Nothing can prepare you for the highs of those first early days of parenthood: the pure wonder of those two tiny babies, the elation and joy that I felt every time I was jolted awake by their cries, as if from a dream ... But now, it was a dream no longer. The babies were all too real. All of that giddy pinch-your-self-it's-so-amazing lasted for a month, maybe two months max ...

Now, the dream had taken a turn and I was just another casualty of parenthood: neck deep in sleep deprivation, human faeces and vomit. Nothing could ever have prepared me for that nightmarish plot twist.

I know it's not the done thing, but if you know someone that is about to have their first baby, frankly, I think you owe it to them to chuck a few truth bombs in their direction:

'Hello, mate, sit yourself down. I'll be honest with you, it's a bit of a horror show. You're never going to finish a cup of tea or coffee again and you're going to have to get used to having a shit with the door open. Your sex life is over, your social life is dead and if you want to have an ice cream, you're going to have to eat it behind a bin in the garden. Anyway, CONGRATULATIONS!'

Nothing can prepare you for the kind of sleep deprivation that comes from a baby, or in our case babies. Neither of us has any idea how we're going to carry on. Surely this torment can't continue indefinitely?

And it's only been a couple of months since our sons were born.

As the babies approached their eight-week milestone, it felt like neither Chloe nor I had slept more than forty-five minutes at a time. My entire life began to unfold like some kind of Dalí-esque dream sequence.

We were just about getting by. There was no escape in any case. We'd gone full Stockholm syndrome and were willingly submitting to this punishment.

Getting to know my sons in those first few months was by far the best and worst time in my life. I can't tell you exactly when my feelings went from being protective of my boys to the out-and-out, 'I would throw myself in front of a bus for you' kind of unqualified love. Nothing discernible happened; it just crept up on me and every day we spent together brought us closer together.

In retrospect, it really wasn't long before our twins began to recognise me, my smell, my voice and then they seemed as happy in my arms as they were in Chloe's. (Except when they were hungry. Then I was dead to them.)

Prior to the birth of my boys, I don't think anyone would have said that I'm good with babies, but I think I was good with our two. I felt confident when I was with them on my own and they in turn seemed to trust me.

As weeks went by, I instinctively recognised the individual cries of my boys and how to comfort them when they were inconsolable. I knew how each of my sons preferred to be held. I was barely able to disguise my discomfort when I handed one of my sons over to a friend or family member and watched as they held him wrong. I'd look on with a fixed smile watching as my son would cry because he didn't feel comfortable or safe.

'It might be better if you just hold him on his front, that's how he likes it,' I'd find myself saying.

'Maybe if you just support his head ...'

'I think I should just take him for a bit.'

I'm not a helicopter mum, OK? I just found it difficult to watch someone manhandle my son while he was screaming his head off.

It's just as well that I did invest in bonding with them, because otherwise I have no idea how I would have put up with the length of every single day. I could remember quite clearly one of the nurses on the maternity ward telling us that the first six weeks were the hardest, but then our babies would settle down and they'd start to sleep for longer periods.

Chloe and I were still clinging onto those words, long after the first six weeks had passed, however.

'She said *six weeks*. After six weeks they would be sleeping for hours, she said that. It's been nine weeks. Why are they not sleeping?'

'It's bullshit! She lied to us! THEY DON'T SLEEP. Why won't they *ever* sleep?'

Friends reassured us that it was in fact after three months that the babies would start sleeping more: by then the babies' stomachs would have grown, they would no longer be quite so hungry, therefore they would sleep for anything up to four hours at a stretch.

At three months, they were still only asleep for an hour at a time and rarely the same hour.

'Oh! It's not three months! Look, this book says six months!'

No, it was not happening at six months either.

'It's a year. They will sleep after a year!'

NOPE! THEY'RE STILL NOT SLEEPING!

Sleep became the most highly prized commodity in our house. That's all I wanted: to lie somewhere horizontally and kip. Night times were the worst. The boys were still in their Moses baskets and we would carry them up to our room when we went to bed. Sometimes, after a bout of wailing, when they'd finally succumbed and fallen asleep, I would lie very still and listen to their breathing, hoping upon hope that they wouldn't wake up. I would feel myself slipping into the deepest, darkest, warmest, bottomless sleep. The kind that envelops you and drags you down with it, the kind of sleep that you think you may never wake from. Just as I started to sink into the depths of this beautiful and all-consuming slumber, I would be jolted back to consciousness by a nerve-jangling noise that could wake the dead:

'Waah! Waah! Waaaaaaaaaaaaaaaaaaaah!!!'

Dragging myself out of that dark, welcoming, soupy sleep pit and back into the harsh reality of a screaming baby or babies, hour after hour after hour, day after day after day, was the closest I've come to understanding what actual torture is. That level of sleep deprivation can drive you mad.

If we had had any idea that it would take two and a half years to get both our boys to sleep through the night, I think I might have just shot myself in the face. Or at the bare minimum, I would have definitely changed my tune and booked a lot more gigs out of town. You know, overnight trips, in places like Aberdeen, for example.

But we didn't know that then, so, with the misguided hope of two clueless parents overwhelmed by lack of sleep and frantically clutching at every straw, we hung on in there.

As first-time parents, we still had no idea what the hell we were doing (panic not, they said, no one does), but in addition, every day felt SO LONG. The days were interminable. They just went on and on and on and on. People with grown-up children told us: 'Enjoy this bit, because it flies by, and you'll be sorry when it's over.'

Firstly, no one is sorry when this bit is over because this bit can feel like hell on earth. Secondly, when your days are twenty-one hours long, they definitely do not feel like they're flying by.

Of course, there were too many best times to mention. The first time they smiled at us knocked us off our feet. The first time they rolled over. The first time they gave a great big belly laugh. The first time they sat up. The first time they figured out that throwing their rattle on to the floor over and over again is the most fun that anyone can have in the entire world and they laughed until they shit themselves. All of that was wonderful.

If you are reading this in the spirit of a bit of ante-natal research, I'm sorry to break it to you, but the day-to-day practical side of looking after a baby is work: actual hard, arduous, punishing, hard *work*. Whatever your state of mind or physical health, you can't have a day off, or a night on your own, you have to just suck it up and get on with it. Your job description, in short, is to be alone all day with what is to all intents and purposes a self-involved, solipsistic, empathy vacuum. Yes, I am talking about babies.

If you are reading this and you have a baby and you are also a person who goes out to work, you need to know that whatever you do when you get there, well, *it isn't work*. It's a holiday.

Long commute? Amazing! You can read a book, listen to a podcast, maybe look out of the window in silence and contemplate your navel. Heavy workload on your desk? Fantastic! You can have a cheeky break and reward yourself with a double-shot latte and triple-choc muffin. Interminable meetings with boring colleagues? Bullseye! Lean back, get comfortable and grab forty winks.

Meanwhile, think about it. Your partner is up to his or her neck in shitty nappies and regurgitated breast milk in sole charge of a screaming baby for long, *long* days that stretch out for what feels like weeks with little to no company or support. So, enjoy your break! And if when you come home after your 'hard day' at the office and long commute and your partner screams:

'I CANNOT DO THIS ANY MORE! YOU TAKE HER! I'M RUNNING MYSELF A BATH AND THERE IS NO BLOODY DINNER SO YOU'LL HAVE TO GET YOURSELF A TAKEAWAY!'

Don't turn to them with a bewildered look on your face and tell them that you only just got in and you are knackered, because they will be justified in throwing a wrought-iron frying pan at your head and no one would judge them for it.

A crying baby is stressful even for the most laid-back of people, of which I am not. I was, however, surprised to discover that with my children I had all the patience of a saint.

It was just as well. The little one, Twin Two, was having a particularly terrible time of it. He was the one who loved sleeping on his front, but he never seemed comfortable. In all the photos of him as a small baby, he is balanced on his front on one of our arms.

He had always been small and even at three months he was still the size of a newborn. His brother was feeding really well and putting on weight, but our little fella was really struggling. He took forever to feed and afterwards he would cry non-stop. The health visitor didn't seem too worried as he was putting on some weight, albeit not as much as we'd hoped. Still, Chloe and I knew that something was not quite right, but we had no idea what it could be.

I took him to our GP, who unfortunately was about as much help and reassurance as a broken finger at a netball match.

'He cries a lot and I think he might be in pain,' I told him.

'He's a baby. Babies cry.'

'I know that, but he's also so small and I don't think he's putting on enough weight.'

'Well, some people are small and some people are big; the same goes for babies.'

I could see he was exasperated with me. In his eyes I was just another overzealous and neurotic new mum who was overreacting to what were perfectly normal symptoms.

I can appreciate that new mums are the bane of the overworked GP, but it's fair to say that we also have something called instinct. Chloe and I *knew* that there was something wrong with him and we didn't feel like we were being heard.

Sitting in our GP's surgery with Twin Two, I saw him roll his eyes as I was speaking and I felt an irresistible urge to stand up, walk over and kick him in the dick. Dear Reader, I resisted. Even now, it feels good to think about doing it, though. I'm not saying I still fantasise about it … OK, yes, I do. I still fantasise about it.

Eventually, he did take the trouble to examine him.

'It's probably reflux.'

'He's not throwing up.'

'Silent reflux. Try giving him these drops in his milk and you'll find it should help.'

It didn't help because it wasn't silent reflux, or colic, or heartburn.

He just kept on crying.

This went on and on for months and nothing seemed to help make him more comfortable. When you are alone with a crying baby, it can send you absolutely batshit mental. It was agonising to see him in such misery. It was also a lot harder to deal with his upset, because we had not one, but two of them to contend with. On the rare occasion that the little one went to sleep, you can bet your bottom dollar that the bigger one picked that precise moment to give his lungs a workout and start bellowing. It was relentless.

Chloe and I were lucky because my work allowed me to be around so much, and if one of us was on the brink, the other could swoop in and take over, but even with two of us pretty much sharing the childcare fifty-fifty it was hard. I don't know how single parents do it. I have no idea how any parent copes on their own. If you are a single parent reading this, you have my undying respect, because you are a bloody champion! Single parents are heroes because they have to be everything to their kids: nurturer, disciplinarian, boundary-maker, educator, listener, supporterer ... I'm pretty sure that last one isn't even a word, but you get my point.

I'm not going to undermine any single dads out there, because any single parent is a bloody hero in my eyes. I just find it interesting that it's single mums who get the brunt of everyone's judgement. As if being a single parent isn't hard enough without being told that you're a bloody burden. You're not. You, reading this right now, you are amazing! In fact, each and every one of you is a bloody marvel and an asset to humanity and guess what, society is wrong and the patriarchy is wrong and I'm going to organise this bloody parade and you're all going to get a free holiday paid for by this shitty government if it kills me![1]

If you have a baby who sleeps, you've struck gold. If you get to sleep for more than four hours at a time on any given night, you're fine, you can handle it. If you have a baby or babies who wake up every hour, every night, for months on end, however, you're buggered. Obviously, you'll survive it, but it's going to be a long old road.

[1] I literally cannot promise any of this, but I stand by the rest of it.

9

Home Sweet Home

Soon after the boys had turned six months old, the lease on our Airbnb was up and we moved back into our (UNFINISHED)[1] house. The day we moved, it was freezing cold. The house hadn't been heated for the entire winter and it was like an icebox. It didn't help that the bottom half of our house was 'open plan', which by the way is code for IMPOSSIBLE TO HEAT.

Neither of us had any idea how to work the central heating. Equipped with a brand-new thermostat that

---

[1] It would be unprofessional of me to go into just how much Chloe and I hated the builders, which is why I've dedicated an entire section in this chapter to do just that.

seemed to have some deep intuition as to how you wanted to heat each room, it would regulate the temperature of every radiator based on ... I don't bloody well know! I STILL DON'T UNDERSTAND THE POXING THING!

Sometimes I think technology is holding us back. There should be grades of technology you want to invest in. I'm definitely not a Luddite, but I'm also not a person who wants to read a manual that is over a hundred pages long on how to heat my house. All I want is a hot radiator, I don't want to have to factor in where I keep the bloody thermostat or how hot it is in the kitchen. Just assume that I want the radiator to be on and boiling hot all the time, until I say otherwise.

The first few days we couldn't get the radiator heat above lukewarm. We spoke to a plumber, who explained in detail that we needed to ensure that each radiator was gradated, so that the further away from the boiler it was, the higher the temperature should be. I remember looking at him thinking we'd never get the hang of this thermostat, and four years later, we still have no actual idea how to heat our home.

We worried about the boys; they were still so small and even though they seemed to radiate heat most of the time, at night we had to wrap them up in extra blankets to keep them warm.

Downstairs in our now cavernous living space, Chlo and I had to use an electric heater to help keep us warm. The bloody thing was practically touching our feet and it just about warmed our knees and nothing else. It also didn't help that the house was far from finished, so it was dusty and cluttered with work tools and materials.

We didn't know this at the time, but it was going to be another seven months before the builders would complete the job. Seven whole months of dust, aggro and having to see our builder's face. Not that there was anything wrong with it. He was OK looking, I suppose. It was just that we had graphic fantasies about his face that usually involved caving it in with a spade.

Living in a building site, or even in a house that constantly has people working on it, can get you down. Particularly as every single thing they did was either not right, not how we wanted it, or made with cheaper materials than the ones we had paid for. I'm not saying all builders are thieving crooks with no moral compass; I'm just saying our one was.

We spent days having to clean the dust from every surface so the boys could play on the floor. The dust seemed to have infested every area of the house. Added to that, most of the house had doors but no handles, or if they did have handles, they were only on one side of the door which made getting in and out of every room feel like the *Crystal Maze*.

On top of this, our house always felt like it was a mess. It's not because we are a couple of slobs, far from it. Chloe is a borderline fascist when it comes to cleanliness and the art of putting stuff away. I, on the other hand, consider myself to be more of a free spirit.

'Are you going to leave your bag there?'

'No, I'll move it in a minute.'

'Well, can you move it now? It's been there for two days and I hate having to look at it every time I walk into the living room.'

'FINE! I'LL MOVE IT! BLIMEY! Since when am I living with Marie Kondo?!'

I wrote that with the intention of illustrating just how annoying Chloe is, but reading it back I can't help feeling I don't come off well either.

The problem wasn't my bag, it was the fact that we were living in a building site. We had spent the first six months of our children's lives in a rented house ten minutes' walk from the house we bought. We had been reassured over and over again that our house would be ready by the time we moved in. It was now eight months later, it was freezing cold and our house was nowhere close to ready.

As I've explained before, Chloe is not an 'emotive' woman. That's not to say that she is not loving and kind and generous and a lot of fun; she is all of these things, she's just a very even woman.

Which is why her reaction and response to our builders was all the more intense. Unlike myself, Chloe doesn't seem to have strong emotions about most people, she likes them, she's not that keen on them, she rarely if ever 'hates' anyone. I, on the other hand, can go from zero to I FUCKING HATE YOU in under ten seconds.

'That bloke driving behind us is right up my arse ... Can you believe this prick? OK, I'm going to slow right down ... Ten miles per hour should do it. See how he likes that! Hey, he's just given me the finger! EAT SHIT AND DIE, YOU MASSIVE WANKER!'

So, you can imagine my surprise when I realised that when it came to the relationship we had with our builder, I was having to play good cop.

'Jen, you're going to have to talk to him. I can't even look at his face. I fantasise about smashing his smug head in with a hammer!'

'Um ... OK, leave the talking to me then.'

Never in the history of my entire life have I had to play the calm, rational mediator. It's not really in my DNA, but guess what? I rose to the challenge and I can honestly say that I maintained my cool throughout.

It's not because I liked the guy, I thought he was a massive bellend too. A bellend who thought that, because we were women, he could patronise and easily manipulate us.

He would swoop in to our home, demanding to pick up one of our precious boys while talking complete bollocks as to why he couldn't get the exact boiler we wanted, or why he'd paved over our garden without asking, or why he had given us a cheap shitty bathroom radiator and charged us for the expensive radiator that we actually wanted.

Radiatorgate is ongoing. There are still days where out of the blue Chloe will blurt out:

'I can't believe we're stuck with this horrible radiator. We should go to his office and throw it through his fucking window!'

'On the plus side we did get the boiler we wanted, so that's a win!'

'OF COURSE WE GOT THE BOILER WE WANTED BECAUSE WE PAID FOR IT, NOT THAT PIECE OF CRAP HE TRIED TO INSTALL. I HATE HIM! I HATE HIM SO MUCH! I WANT TO STICK HIS HEAD IN A CEMENT MIXER ...'

It's been over four years but the wounds still run deep.

Having work done on your home is a stressful and emotional time, never mind when you're doing it with two small babies. Also, while I could help Chlo liaise with the builder I was of little to no use when it came to deciding on anything in the house. On any occasion when I did try to give some input, it became clear that it was never quite right:

'You need to help me choose where to put the plugs in the living room.'

'Right, um ... Well, how about if we have one there?'

'No, the sofa will go there.'

'I thought it was going there ...'

'No, Jen! We talked about this. The TV will go there.'

'So, put two plugs here then ...'

'The TV is going to hang on the wall so unless you want a three-foot extension cable hanging off the wall ...'

'OH MY GOD! YOU DECIDE THEN!'

It's hard to stay motivated when most of your suggestions are perpetually wrong. Fortunately for me, Chlo seemed happier when I wasn't putting in my two penn'orth.

I like to tell people we're in an equal relationship but all the evidence definitely leans to the contrary.

Six and a half months in, and the lack of sleep was by now so horrendous that we had to take some practical action in order to make it feel like we were vaguely in control. The boys' bedroom, in contrast to most of the rest of the house, was finished, and it had a working radiator. We decided, therefore, that it was time for the boys to move out of their Moses baskets, out of our bedroom and into their cots in their own room.

At this point, this felt like a move forward. We were no longer jangled awake by every snuffle, cough or cry. This was a brilliant idea.

Or was it?

All we had done was put our two sons in another room that meant that when they cried, I had further to walk to get to them. There were nights when I was wakened by the sound of crying, every bone in my body aching, the very essence of my exhausted soul weighing me down as I attempted to drag my shattered body out of our deliciously warm bed.

I'd stagger into their room to find an awake and distressed baby, lift him out of his cot and hold him, rocking him gently, whispering in his ear to calm him, walking round and round the bedroom until his cries lessened, his breathing calmed and it felt like he might be asleep. I would carefully place him back in his cot, creep out of their room and back into my bed where I would fall back to sleep almost instantly. Then, in less than an hour, 'Waah! Waah! Waaaaaaaaaaaaaaaaaaaaah!!!' and I was woken AGAIN, this time by the other one. And, so it would go on ALL NIGHT.

There were nights where I found myself on my knees in their room, close to tears, begging for them to, 'PLEASE just sleep!' It's a testament to how much we love those boys that we put up with it.

I'm amazed that we managed to get anything done on so little sleep, but needs must and I was now working every weekend. There's no doubt that we struggled. Even the sparkle in Chloe's eyes had begun to dim. Every now and again, I had to stay over for one or two nights in a hotel. Boy, did I make the most of those occasional hotel rooms. Damn right I did. I was having the full Lenny Henry experience.

I was aware, however, that it was probably best not to over-egg that particular pudding, given that Chloe was stuck at home with two screaming babies.

'How is Birmingham?'

'Oh, it's a nightmare. I'm having a terrible time ...'

'Being in a hotel must be nice?'

'No, it's ... it's ... awful. The bed is so ... lumpy. Awful. You'd hate it.'

Even those brief respites were not enough to replenish my sapped energy levels. I was barely conscious, which, paradoxically, had its plus side. Too exhausted to give anything much lucid thought, I turned up to my gigs with little to no expectation or ego. I would arrive, chug whatever caffeinated drink was available, do the gig and leave. As a result, probably because I cared a lot less, my gigs were going a lot better. I didn't care what the audience thought, or my peers thought. I just needed to get through the show so I could go back to my hotel, get into my bed, and sleep, glorious sleep.

Meanwhile, Chloe was googling the Google out of Google, trying to work out what might be wrong with our little son. The search history on her laptop revealed that the answer to 'causes and treatments for near-continual wailing' was cranial massage. So that was the next magic wand that Chloe decided to try. For the record, I thought it was a load of old bollocks.

'Why are we taking him for cranial massage?'

'Because Jen, I googled "near-continual wailing" and it said it might actually help him! He's in pain and it said that lots of babies benefit from cranial massage.'

'What's the point of it?'

'Some babies have traumatic births and their heads get stuck in the birth canal and it can cause damage that cranial massage can help with and …'

'They were born by caesarean, so they can't have got their heads trapped …'

'Look, we're just doing it, OK?'

We did it and to be fair, it didn't seem to do him any harm, but it didn't do much good either. Even the cranial masseur felt that his crying had nothing to do with his neck or spine and a lot more to do with his stomach.

So, we were back at the beginning, none the wiser and finding it difficult to know who to ask for help.

By this point the boys were seven months old. The little one's cries were becoming more and more distressed. We had one freak night where we got to sleep for a whole two hours! Chloe and I actually high-fived one another. We were ecstatic! I sometimes still think about that night.

Was this the start of them sleeping for longer? Were we finally going to get something resembling a reprieve? No. It was a one-off, and not to be repeated for at least another six months.

Chloe had been on Google again, and it was her idea to get a sleep trainer, something that I acutely resented with every fibre of my being. I can't explain why, but the thought of inviting a stranger into my house to tell me what I should or shouldn't be doing to help my children sleep really put my nose out of joint. After all, what the hell did she know? We were the parents. Surely we would know more than she does? Right? Why are you looking at me like that? OK, fine. No, we didn't really know what to do. Yes, I am a stubborn twat.

Chloe booked our first session with the sleep trainer. I was working that night, so I arrived home late from my gig to find this woman I'd never met in the boys' bedroom. I was immediately annoyed.

'What is she doing in there?'

'Can you keep your voice down? She's helping our boys sleep.'

'Well, I don't know how she's supposed to know more about our children than we do.'

'Because she's trained in this!'

'Oh yeah? What's she got? A PhD in sleeping babies? I didn't realise that was a thing.'

'Do you want to sleep in the loft?'

'There isn't a bed in the loft. Oh, I see … No thank you.'

I didn't get up at 6am the following morning to get the feedback on how the boys slept. I was just enjoying five solid hours of uninterrupted sleep. The upshot of one night with the sleep trainer was that the little one was not sleeping because he was in pain.

YES, WE KNEW THAT!

Chloe was so upset. Even though we had known all along that there was something very wrong with our little Twin Two, it wasn't until Chloe heard it from another person that she felt both vindicated and guilty. She immediately felt like a terrible mother and that she had fallen short as a parent, whereas when I feel criticised or undermined, I go on the defensive.

'What the hell does that bloody woman know? She spent one night with him and now she's the fount of all wisdom? It's not like we haven't taken him to the GP four times! We've tried all the drugs for every possible problem from colic to bloody heartburn and none of it worked. She's not even a doctor! I think it's a bloody con and you should have told her to stick her opinions up her arse!'

The sleep trainer said that it was very likely that our son was allergic to Chloe's breast milk. Or rather the dairy protein in her milk. Had Chloe tried not eating dairy? It might take four to six weeks for it to leave her body, so in the meantime maybe she could go to the doctor to get a dairy-free milk formula.

'What is she on about? How can he be allergic to breast milk? I've never heard of a baby who is allergic to his mother's milk. Dr Bloody Sleep Trainer PhD doesn't know what she's talking about!'

Chloe ignored my rants and went all proactive. She booked an appointment to take him back to the GP and this time she wasn't taking no for an answer.

Our GP, as I've described, already thought I was an irrational, hysterical helicopter parent with no objectivity about my children's health. Chloe, however, had no such relationship with him. She also had the ability in difficult situations to be assertive and assured without sounding like she was going to get physically violent.

Some people might say that Chloe's approach is better than mine, but I don't like to admit I'm wrong, so you won't be hearing that from me. It's no surprise then, that her appointment with our GP was a hell of a lot more fruitful than my previous three visits.

At some point as a parent, new or not so new, you're going to have to stand your ground, whether it be with a doctor, a health visitor or a crotchety nurse. Yes, they have knowledge, but what they lack is your instinct about your child. If you really feel like something is wrong, then you have to keep calm, and keep going back until you get them to listen. Chloe did just that:

'I think he's allergic to milk protein.'[1]

'What makes you think that?'

'He's in pain. I can tell he's in pain and I would like to try putting him on a dairy-free formula. I believe you can prescribe that.'

'I don't think that's available on the NHS.'

'Well, I'd like you to look into it and, if it *is* available, send me a prescription.'

'You may find that's something you need to buy yourself privately.'

'Well, as I said, I'd like you to look into it and if it is possible, hopefully you can send me a prescription.'

Fast-forward two weeks and a prescription for special dairy-free formula magically arrives at our local pharmacy.

CHLOE WINS! IN YOUR FACE, DOCTOR ROBOT MAN!

It worked wonders. The formula was called Nutramigen and smelled so dreadful, I couldn't imagine how bad it would taste, but the little lad LOVED it, and now that he was feeding from a bottle, we could see exactly how much he was having. He fed without crying and he started to put on weight again. I cannot tell you how quickly we noticed a change. He was no longer in pain. At last.

---

[1] Cue obligatory eye-rolling, huge sigh and passive-aggressive tone.

You're probably thinking that I should really be thanking our sleep trainer and I would have, really. I would have thanked her and sent her a bottle of the finest champagne[2] ... had they started SLEEPING!

They didn't. Argh.

Not long after we had moved back in, we came home one night to discover that the heating wasn't working. Every radiator was ice cold and we could see our breath as we walked through the house. Being cold is bloody miserable and debilitating and when you have two six-month-old babies in tow, it's a FRICKIN' NIGHTMARE.

We headed straight for the boiler, which is located in our loft conversion. You know, the room that isn't finished yet. Yeah, that room. On entering, Chloe quickly opened the cupboard where our boiler lives, fiddled with knobs and bits and bobs (I don't know, I don't have a practical bone in my body) and voila, the boiler fires up.

'Oh, thank God. It's like an icebox in here!' [Head still in the boiler cupboard.]

'Whatever you do, don't shut the bedroom door because there's no handle on this side of it.'

'I know! I'm not completely stupid!'

You and I both know that isn't true.

---

[2] I obviously mean Prosecco.

By this time, I am currently entertaining our two sons on the floor of our loft bedroom, watching them crawling about and trying to make sure they don't put every last thing they pick up into their mouths. I'm also conscious that they are very near the door and I don't want them rolling out and falling down a flight of uncarpeted stairs.

Better shut the door.

'Jen, did you just shut the door?'

'Yes, I did. I don't want the boys falling down the stairs!'

'WHY DID YOU DO THAT?'

' … Instinct?'

'You've just locked us in!'

'We're not locked in, I'll get us out …' (panicking) 'Chlo. We're locked in.'

'JESUS CHRIST, JEN! WHAT DID I LITERALLY JUST SAY TO YOU? "DO NOT SHUT THE DOOR!" AND WHAT DO YOU DO? YOU SHUT THE BLOODY DOOR! SO NOW WE'RE TRAPPED UP HERE AND WE CAN'T GET OUT! HONESTLY, WHAT IS THE ACTUAL POINT OF YOU?'

'Don't panic! We can phone for help.'

'I don't have my phone with me, do you?'

'No, it's downstairs …'

'AAAAAAARGH! HOW THE FUCK ARE WE GOING TO GET OUT? WE'RE STUCK UP HERE! WITH NO WATER AND NO FOOD!'

'At least you can feed the boys with your boobs.'

At this point, I think it's fair to say that there was now a heightened air of panic in the locked room. Having told you that Chloe doesn't do emotions, I realise I am now only relating incidents where she is 100 per cent emoting. Maybe that's why I remember them so clearly. I also think that it's fair to say that between the two of us, I was definitely the calmer one in this situation. I think this came with being the person that had royally ballsed up – you're not allowed to be responsible for a catastrophe *and* have a complete breakdown.

It's at times like this, when you are up against what at first appears to be a catastrophic situation with no way out, that you realise just how resourceful you can be.

'Well, we could wait until the builders come ...'

'It's Friday. The builders aren't coming back until Monday.'

'What if we shout out the window?'

'It's a Velux window, Jen. No one will hear you and even if they do, they can't see you and even if they see you, how are they going to get into our house to let us out?'

'I could try climbing out of the window and ...'

'Oh, for fuck's sake, SHUT UP!'

It was tense; the reality of our situation did not take long to dawn on both of us. We were currently trapped in a room with no food and no running water, no phones, no means of contacting anyone to let them know that we were prisoners of our own loft conversion.

'At least we got the boiler working.'

'That would be a bonus if we had A WORKING RADIATOR IN THIS ROOM, YOU ABSOLUTE MORON!'

It was starting to get personal.

I can't say that I felt too great about myself in that moment. To all intents and purposes, I had deliberately trapped us in a room with no way of escape. My usually unflappable partner was looking seriously panicked, not because she was worried about the two of us, but more how she was going to keep the boys fed, warm and watered in a room for forty-eight hours with no heating, no blankets, beds ... You get the idea.

My instinct, particularly when I'm the idiot who's messed up, is to try and make light of the situation. Find some humour in the moment, break the tension with a laugh ...

'It could be worse. We could be stuck in here with the builder!'

I don't think I need to describe the look that Chloe gave me in that moment. But, let's just say that if looks could kill, my body would have spontaneously exploded and splattered unceremoniously around our new loft conversion.

In many ways I am useless at absolutely everything. I can change a hoover bag, or a lightbulb, and possibly a fuse in a plug, but that's it. If I'm required to assemble furniture, fix anything, construct Lego, put up shelves, open a Kinder Surprise, you can forget it.

The only way I was ever going to live down this latest exhibition of uselessness was if I managed to get us out of there. And soon. Sure, there wasn't a handle on our side of the door, but all I needed was something I could stick inside it to twist it, and then I could get us out. By this point Chloe was focusing her energy on being furious with me and other pressing concerns:

'I just don't understand how you could be so bloody stupid! I told you not to close the door and then you closed the bloody door. It's like you did it on purpose. I don't know if I have enough breast milk to feed both of them for two days, they need food as well and all the pouches are downstairs ...'

Meanwhile, I had found a biro that one of the builders had left behind and using my initiative (yes, you heard that correctly), I stuck the pen in the hole where the handle should be and, turning it slowly ... OPEN SESAME! I managed to open the door!

Please, don't applaud me! OK: go right ahead, applaud me.[3]

---

[3] I'm a stand-up comedian. I have no idea if I'm succeeding at anything without laughter or some kind of ovation.

You would think in that moment that Chloe might have acknowledged my success in releasing us from our temporary imprisonment, or possibly a flash of remorse for fantasising about murdering me for the last half an hour. Sadly, *not*.

'How did you get the door open?'

'I used the pen and...'

'Never mind. Let's just get the hell out of here before you close the bloody door again. You're lucky we got out, I was about to kill you.'

I know she loves me really.

Unfortunately, my reputation precedes me, so if that story is ever retold, not only am I the person to lock us in, Chloe is currently the one that miraculously got us out. The more I protest, the more people believe her version of the story.

The truth is, faced with an indignant Chloe or this idiot, who are you going to believe?

Which is why it's important to write a detailed book proposal, find a literary agent, meet with a publisher and get a book deal, just so you can get your version down in print.

I win.

10

Feeding Time

No sooner had we got to the bottom of the dairy allergy mystery, and it was all change *again*. At eight months, the boys were ready to be weaned.

Imagine you have someone who has exclusively been fed on something delicious and warm and sweet that they can either suck out of a breast or a bottle. They love it. They can't get enough of it, and now you have to slowly take that away from them and introduce actual, solid, real-life food to that someone. Then imagine how frustrating it is when every single delicious thing you lovingly prepare, solely for their good and their delectation, is either ignored, thrown on the floor or violently spat out in your face.

Now imagine attempting this feat with the conflicting advice of every mother and baby book, parent, grandparent and well-meaning observer who happens to walk by.

'The best way to wean your baby is baby-led weaning. I just place finger food in front of her and then she chooses what she wants to eat.'

'I just think if you puree organic vegetables or fruit, then you know what they're eating and how much ...'

'I don't cook separate food for the children. Dylan has been eating chicken jalfrezi since he was eight months old!'

Well, for what it's worth, after trying it with our two for a week, I thought they should do their own bloody shopping and then cook their own dinner and see how quickly they throw THAT on the floor!

Weaning is its own private hell.

Chloe and I were agreed that we were going to make all our baby meals from scratch. There would be no nasty shop-bought packet food for our boys! Why? Because we adore them too much, they deserve to have only the finest, purest, healthiest, freshest hand-selected ingredients, and as Earth Mamas we love nothing more than cooking all day every day, comparing recipes with other mums and Instagramming our meals to share the wealth of our knowledge on nutrition and ... Fuck me, I've lost the will to live already.

We both went on mother and baby food blogs, reading recipe after recipe and article after article written by women photographed grinning next to toddlers who are plainly *loving* their roasted vegetable tagine with couscous.

'At first Theo wouldn't touch quinoa but I found that after three attempts he's a quinoa convert! Now he signs for me to make it most days ...'

Really? REALLY? Your kid LIKES quinoa? Sod off.

Who has time to spend the day thinking up recipes, photographing them, sticking a filter on top and then endlessly bragging online all day every day about how much your baby eats and how much they love your cheeky sweetcorn fritters?

We tried, Lord knows we tried. The thing with babies is, they can lull you into a false sense of security. The first time Twin Two tried avocado, he loved it! In fact, he couldn't get enough of it. So, we gave him another spoonful, and another, and another. Five minutes later and he projectile-vomited every last ounce of that avocado all over himself, his high chair and a good expanse of surrounding surface area. He didn't touch an avocado for another year.

We spent weeks pureeing sweet potatoes, avocados, peas and butternut squash, broccoli and banana, spinach and apple. We stuck it in ice cube trays, we sliced up carrots, red pepper and cucumber and anything else they could hold in their hand

and munch on. We TRIED but after watching every single meal end up coating the wall, we buggered off to the supermarket to increase the share price of a particular brand of baby food (we all know which one) for the next six months. If they were going to reject their food, I'd rather it came out of an over-priced pouch of organic something or other, than my hard graft.

I couldn't keep up with what they liked and didn't like from one day to the next. They liked a meal one minute, they HATED it the next. What was that about? I'm not saying I want to eat the same food every day, but if you leave a gap of a week, I'll probably eat it again and if someone else has cooked it, I'll be bloody grateful. Not my two. OH NO. Every time we put food in front of them, it was like the National Lottery Thunderball. If you have a baby who isn't fussy with their food, I'm telling you, thank the GODS. Not only did our two never sleep, now they barely ate.

Even after we got through the weaning phase and they were on full-on solids, they continued to torment us with their fussy eating. It was this, more than anything, that stressed me out. And, given how stressful it is having two babies who never sleep, that's saying something.

Chlo and I were already neurotic about how small they both were, so for us, feeding your children was one of the most fundamental things we could do to make sure they were healthy and growing. Admittedly, the bigger one had caught up a bit and was now about average in terms of his weight and height, but the little one was still very little. It's not like he wasn't growing, he was, and he was growing at a rate that, I suppose, was in line with the weight he was born, but we wanted him to exceed that rate, to have a growth spurt and at least catch up with his slightly beefier brother. The last thing we wanted was for him to stay small forever. If we couldn't feed him, well, what kind of shitty parents were we?

Chloe cannot cope with throwing food away. I sometimes think she was born in the wrong era, because she would have been perfect during the war. I genuinely think she'd have loved rationing, eating powdered eggs and raw suet and making beef dripping and wood chip sandwiches for the family. The very idea that we have access to this much food and can store it in a fridge overwhelms her, let alone to have it and then not eat every last morsel of it.

It doesn't matter how out of date something is, or how long it's been in the cupboard or fridge, in Chloe's opinion, we should eat it. If I am away for any amount of time and haven't left an actual meal cooked and ready for her, she'll just pick random things from the fridge and that will be her dinner.

'What did you eat tonight, love?'

'Well, you didn't cook so I had to have that quiche we didn't finish on Sunday with a half-eaten boiled egg the boys didn't want and some left-over cabbage.'

Eat your heart out, *MasterChef*.

For Chloe, cooking requires hours of preparation and thought; she can't just rustle something together – well, she can but you wouldn't want to eat it. I like to make stuff up. Chlo likes to know exactly what she is cooking, have every single ingredient and plenty of time to make it. I like to wing it and hope for the best.[1]

The one thing Chloe and I do have in common is how little we enjoyed making food for our boys when they were weaning. It was painful to spend hours cooking, only to find yourself scraping it into the bin an hour later, or watch them sick it up the second after you spooned it into their mouth.

I'm not saying that I'm a great cook, in fact no one's saying that. But I can cook and I can make the basics and sometimes something more than basic and on the whole people (Chloe) seem to enjoy it. My kids? Not so much.

Once they were fully weaned and on full-on solids, I made them a variety of meals – anything from a fish pie, chicken and apple balls, spaghetti bolognaise, vegetable soups, even a Thai curry. Each time they looked

---

[1] The way we approach cooking perfectly sums up our respective personalities.

at me like I was offering them a coughed-up hairball that I'd just pulled out of the vacuum cleaner.

Every single meal time went a bit like this:

'Come on, darling, Mama's cooked you a lovely dinner and if you eat it all up Mama will give you a yoghurt!'

(I don't know if speaking in the third person helps but I've seen other parents do it and I appear to be committed to it now.)

Suffice to say, confronted with my lovely dinner, my son would look at me with a face that clearly said, 'I'm not eating that muck.' And in case there was any ambiguity in his expression, I would watch the plate fly off the table and my lovely dinner land face down on the floor. Dinner that I had just cooked, dinner that I had lovingly prepared, dinner that had the right amount of protein, carbohydrates and vegetables to provide a balanced diet for our son. A dinner that would hopefully help his bones and brain grow because he's small, he's a small lad and I want him to grow so he has to EAT. WHY WON'T HE EAT MY DINNER?

To anyone who has tried to negotiate with an eight-month-old, I would just say this: save your breath – they're not interested. And if you're trying to negotiate anything, make sure you have more than a raspberry yoghurt up your sleeve, because as far as bribes go, it has a pretty poor take-up rate.

11

Out and About

Now that the babies were eight months old and crawling up the walls, it was increasingly difficult to find ways to keep them contained and amused at home all day. I needed to get them out of the house, for the sake of everyone's health and safety, not to mention the family's sanity. They needed fresh air and exercise, a change of scenery, and perhaps it was time that they were exposed to some other babies their own age.

It's a lonely business being the primary carer, and on the days I was on my own with the children, I was starting to go up the walls too. Stuck inside with the boys during the day, and although I'm normally allergic to chit-chat with new people, I started to think that despite my aversion to small talk, some adult company other than Chloe would do me good too.

It was time to properly get to grips with the outside world.

Before I could even think about pacing the streets, however, my first challenge was to get the babies out of the house. But first, there was a buggy to contend with.

With one baby, you're laughing. The new single-occupancy buggies and prams are so light and streamlined they're a doddle to manoeuvre. Our double buggy, however, was often wider than the actual pavement. It was a bloody nightmare to get it out of our front door, never mind trying to get it down the street.

We are lucky living in Brighton because, as long as you are prepared for the assault of plentiful and ver-tiginously steep hills, you can pretty much walk everywhere. I don't know how we'd have managed, though, had we still lived in London, particularly with the buggy we had. It had actual tyres that, naturally, got frequent punctures, which meant I was often pushing a buggy up one of the hills with two babies, a load of shopping hanging from it, and a flat tyre. If nothing else, I told myself, it was great for my glutes.

We'd got the buggy second-hand, and from the get-go bits of it were falling apart. It was hard to rock a

'I've-totally-got-this' look when the hood of one of the buggy's chairs kept collapsing into the bigger one's face. I'd hear a muffled cry and think, 'WHAT NOW?', then look down to see him sitting there with the black hood covering his head. Who knows how long I'd been powering down the street with him crying for help before I'd noticed it.

It was no easy feat to maintain a 'serene' look with a buggy that resembled something that might have been used during the last moon landing, much as I tried to pull it off.

Before the birth of our boys I used to be easily irritated by people with kids and I'm ashamed to say that I found women with buggies were the worst.

'Don't mind me! You just take up THE ENTIRE PAVEMENT and I'll take my life into my own hands by stepping on to the road to let you past!'

Well, that woman is definitely me now. I can see the look of utter contempt on people's faces, as I try to navigate my spaceship on wheels and they're obliged to let me past; I smile and thank them, occasionally widening my eyes to assure them I'm aware of the inconvenience. Often nothing is said; every so often I may even get a smile, but more often than not they look like they're about to throw their shopping in my face and I can hear a muttering under the breath:

'How much space do you need … ?'

'Don't mind me …'

'For fuck's sake!'

I almost always ignore these comments because I'm a better person and I can empathise with their frustration. How are they to know what it's like for me, driving that great space tank about the place all day? On one occasion, however, as a young woman muttered a series of fairly abusive insults under her breath, I took umbrage and lost it with her: 'What do you want me to do, love? Transport them by hoverboard? Roll them into a ball and kick them down the street? Fly them overhead attached to a kite? THEY'RE BABIES! This is how we move them!'

She looked at me like I was certifiable: I suddenly realised she had actually been talking to her mate on the phone. I had to pretend I hadn't noticed that small detail, and walked on.

I'm not going to beat myself up about it: I challenge anyone to look calm after pushing a buggy about for eight miles in the pissing rain on four hours' sleep.

Once you do make it out the door and down the street, the next question is where to go. Ideally, as I said, I mainly left the house in the hope of tracking down some adult company. If I'd tried all the usual suspects and didn't have any mates around, the main options available to me on my outings were: parks, cafes and mother and baby groups. Or, in reality, when I factored in the weather (bleak), and finances (I could no longer justify boshing a fortune on flat whites), that just left mother and baby groups. Watching a woman dance around with a puppet of a giraffe (that could do with a good wash), singing 'The Wheels on the Bus', was routinely my only entertainment all day. If you've never been to a mother and baby group then you're basically winning at life, because even the good ones made me want to slip into a coma. (I also know that I said that I usually hated being confronted with people I didn't really know, but I was desperate, OK?)

Sitting there, in a circle with a load of other mums, baby signing to 'Wind the Bobbin Up' as our babies slept through, oblivious, I have to say, I did often find myself questioning all my life choices.

At my regular mother and baby, my 'local', so to speak, there was always one well-meaning woman in her seventies who came round with a plate of rich tea biscuits.

'Would Mum like a tea or coffee?'

'No, Mum would like a large gin, a couple of tramadol, or a crack pipe. Something to soften the edges of this never-ending day.'

I tried, I really did.

There was a music group I persisted in going to, even though I hated it and the boys didn't seem to have a great time there either.

It was run by an older woman who had the voice of someone with a sixty-a-day habit, and a face that said, 'Mess with me, and I will cut you.' Her music group, however, was really popular; in fact, she ran several groups a day for different ages and they were always packed. It probably helped that the room was tiny, but, even so, all the other people there seemed to love it.

I'm not entirely sure why, but she had a different musical student from week to week. He, and it was nearly always a 'he', would accompany her on the piano or guitar as she sang her songs. He would inevitably be doing it wrong,

'Kevin! What on earth are you doing? Are you tone-deaf? It sounds like you're playing the guitar with your feet!'

The poor young bloke would smile and carry on as if he had no choice but to sit there and take a public and humiliating ear-bashing from a formidable woman with a fuse as short as her breath.

I'm not saying she didn't have good ideas, but everything felt rushed and cramped and once the boys were eight months old, they were crawling all over the place, picking things up putting it in their mouths. Enamoured with anything colourful or shiny, they were like two tiny magpies. It became clear that, while she obviously succeeded in running these packed-out mother and baby music sessions, there was one problem: and the thing was, that she *really* had a problem with babies and toddlers. They really got her goat.

'Whose son is this? Could you hold him please? He's not supposed to touch that!'

I'm not usually intimidated by people, but this woman scared the crap out of me. She would bring out this tatty-looking puppet that would supposedly sing along to a song that no one had ever heard of, and all either of my two wanted to do was pet that manky puppet. You'd think this sort of thing must happen all the time, but it used to drive her mad.

'No! NO! Don't touch him like that. OK, I will come to you. I said, I WILL COME TO YOU!'

He's eight months old, love, good luck trying to reason with him about anything. His cognition is limited.

I persisted in going, partly because when it came to their random naps, the time was always convenient, and partly because I was too lonely and cynical and lazy to find anything better to do with them, or with myself. I had only myself to blame.

The other mother and baby group I made myself go to was held in a large church. Now, whatever your opinion about religion and all that jazz, one thing I will say is that they gave up their entire church every week to have a veritable biblical swarm of atheist mums turn up with their babies to play for FREE, glug down their FREE tea and coffee, and feed their kids with FREE snacks. In so many ways, it was great and yet in so many other ways, it was HELL ON EARTH.

Picture it: this church is humongous. Even so, the place was so packed full of mums and babies and toddlers that, for a start, even trying to park our monster of a buggy among all the others to just get into the church was a stress fest. Once inside, sweating, with the two boys in tow, I was overwhelmed by the number of people, wondering how I'd ever find a place to sit. Plus, I was trying to make my way through the throng, holding two wriggling babies who were desperate to get on the floor and start exploring.

In case I haven't made this clear already, by this point both my boys were no longer static; they liked to move and they rarely liked to move in the same direction. Trying to get them to take an interest in the same toys was virtually impossible – while I was busy fishing something out of the little one's mouth or stopping him from stealing a toy from another child, the other one would have buggered off. I would then spend the next five minutes frantically looking around me to see where the hell he had got to. *He can't have got far, can he? He's only a baby, he can't even walk yet!*

Inevitably one of them, and they took this in turns, would be under a table chewing on a Pritt Stick, or standing up, wobbling next to a table leg and inexplicably trying to lick it. I don't know why they did that, they just liked licking table legs, OK?

On more than one occasion a well-meaning volunteer would be holding one of them aloft, a look of mild concern on her face as she scanned the crowd of mothers to see who would come forward to claim him.

It was a humbling experience, every time. I'd make my walk of shame over to her to retrieve him from her, as she stood patiently with that special look on her face: a mixture of sympathy and all-out judgement, the expression of one who no doubt has had children of her own that would never have been left to wander off like that.

OH NO. Not her children. Only idiots like me would do that.

In my defence, there was always a lot going on at any given moment. As soon as I stepped through the door I had to take off their jackets, puddle suits, hats, mittens, and find somewhere to stuff them. They usually both started howling as I did this. I'd lift one up; he'd have done a massive poo. Now I had to find the changing mat, nappies, wipes, cream, and carry both of them to find the changing toilet. I'd find it; as usual, it would be engaged, so then I'd wait, trying to ignore the pitying looks as one or both screamed his head off.

That was the easy part. Once in the changing toilet, that's when the 'fun' started. Don't have kids? Ever wondered why the toilet with the baby changing facilities is engaged for what feels like hours? Here's a brief run down as to why.

OK. Here we go. Firstly, I have to get BOTH of them on the changing table and try to change the one with the dirty nappy and simultaneously try to stop the other one from falling off. I put Mr Dirty-Nappy on his back, take off his nappy to reveal absolute carnage: the poo has escaped out the back of the nappy and is half way up his back. There is poo EVERYWHERE. I'm going to have to completely change him, but I can't because I've LEFT THE BAG WITH HIS CHANGE OF CLOTHES IN THE BAG IN THE BOTTOM OF THE BUGGY!

Sod it, I think: I'll just undress him and change him later. So, I peel off his shit-caked clothes, simultaneously trying to stop the other one from putting his hand in the nappy full of poo, throw the shitty baby grow on the floor – I'll deal with that in a minute. I have managed to clean his bottom, but the poo all the way up his back is the consistency of a broken digestive biscuit – it doesn't seem to matter how much I try to wipe it clean, now I'm essentially just spreading bits of mealy shit all over him. I give up, and wrangle a clean nappy on to his bottom. The same mealy excrement is all over my hands and under my nails. My face is now prickling with sweat, and I have to fight the urge to wipe my brow with my shitty fingers. The other one has got hold of the wet wipes and is pulling them out one by one and throwing them on the floor. My stress levels amp up another level. I try

153

to stuff the wet wipes back in the flap, but it's not working, and the ones that I've stuffed back are now covered in grainy poo. I realise I've forgotten to put nappy cream on his bottom, so I open up the nappy again squeeze out a load of cream and smear it summarily all over his mealy shitty bum. I close the nappy back up, look up and see that meanwhile the other one has grabbed the nappy cream and squeezed most of it on to himself, the table and the wall. Breathe. Breathe. In through the nose, and slowly out through the mouth. I have one naked baby and a handful of shitty clothes, another baby covered in cream, a floor covered in wet wipes and I'm losing the will to live. I take a slightly shitty wet wipe from the pack and try to wipe some of the nappy cream off the second baby, but end up smearing it on a larger surface area. I use the sleeve of my jumper, immediately regret it, now I have nappy cream all over myself. I get the overflowing nappy into a nappy bag and into the bin ignoring the fact that I now have poo all over my fingers again. Overwhelmed, sweating, red-faced and on the brink of screaming, I try to calmly stuff what's left of the cream and the wipes back into the changing bag. I pick up the babies, one of whom is completely naked apart from his nappy.

It's nearly over. With poo-ey, greasy nappy-creamed fingers, I manage to unlock the door. Breathe, and step outside, avoiding eye contact with the woman going in, and the queue of irritated mothers with stinking babies that has formed behind her. I hear someone calling for me, turn around. It's the woman who has just gone in after me. She is pointing at a baby grow caked in shit on the ground:

'Is this yours?'

'Um … No. I don't know whose that is.'

I walk off, vowing never to leave the house again.

12

Unwanted Opinions

First, a disclaimer: I am naturally allergic to other people's opinions at the best of times, but after the boys were born, my intolerance reached pathological proportions.

When the boys were newborn babies, I felt like I was given unwanted advice like it was going out of fashion. When I first ventured out to the park, or mother and baby groups or cafes, I avoided eye contact with anyone. I couldn't bear the endless questions and looks of earnest compassion from other mothers. Even small talk felt loaded with dark meaning. I'd get into a conversation with someone that was so bland that I would be lulled into a false sense of calm. Then somehow, I'd suddenly feel obliged to account for my existential purpose in life.

'Twins! I don't know how you do it. I struggle with just one! Gosh. I can't imagine giving birth to two! Good for you.'

Most of the time, especially when they were tiny, I didn't have the energy to explain. I was so desperate for the small talk to end that I decided not to correct them in case it fired off a whole new volley of questions. I couldn't be arsed with that, so I'd just tell them:

'Oh, it was a dream birth, actually. They just slid out. It was completely pain-free.'

OK, I never said that, but I really wanted to.

Other times, I felt obliged to explain my relationship to my children, because I want my family to be visible and I don't want my boys to feel any embarrassment or shame about having 'different' parents.

'I'm not their mum. I mean I am … I'm just not their biological mum. I'm their non-biological mum. We're not detergent! Ha ha … What I mean is. I didn't give birth to them. My partner did. She's not here.'

Oh God. PLEASE SHUT UP. See what I mean?

I don't know why this was such an issue for me, it's not like I felt any insecurity about my feelings for my children: I think it was more that I was embarrassed that I was calling myself a mum without having gone through any of the tough stuff that every biological mother has gone through.

Even with innocuous, inane mother-and-baby-group chit-chat, I'd inevitably end up plunging further down that particular sinkhole:

'It's so cold, isn't it?' I'd be asked.

'Yeah, it's cold alright ...' I'd reply.

'I've had to take blankets out for the kids; another thing to carry – it's a nightmare! Are those your boys?'

'Yes.'

'I've definitely seen them around at other groups.'

'That's possible, I don't always go with them.'

'Oh! I must have seen them with their dad ...'

'Yeah, you might have seen him. He's short, about five foot two, blonde and a woman.'

Again, I'd never say that, naturally. I'm never passive-aggressive or rude when people make assumptions and think that I'm either the biological mum or have a husband.

I know it's the twenty-first century and we're all so forward-thinking and right-on and blah blah blah, but the fact is our family is still outside of what is considered the 'norm'. Consequently, unlike most parents, I'm constantly having to explain/justify my situation as the 'other mum'; it's like I have to 'come out' all over again.

If you're gay, you'll already be acutely aware of this, so this is just for my straight readers. 'Coming out', isn't something I had to do once in my life to friends and family, because, in fact, I have to do it almost every day and it can be emotionally draining. It doesn't matter how much you love your children, but these constant reminders that you're not your child's 'proper mum' can wear you down if you let them.

If you're not the 'other' parent it might be helpful for you to know that your partner is having to handle these emotional and practical issues. It's likely they haven't expressed any of this to you, but I speak from experience: the 'other' prefix can be a bit of a burden.

Every time I took them out and had to negotiate the pair of them in public, someone would always come over.

Once, when they were very small, I took them to a cafe near my house. They were both crying, and I was coping as best as I could: changing their nappies on a chair next to me, wrestling with a flask to pour the expressed milk into so I could feed them. A woman eventually approached me.

'Hi, I'm sorry but my friends and I have been watching you for ages and I just wanted to say ...' she started.

Oh God, please don't say it ...

' ... we think you're an absolute hero! We've only got a baby each, we can't imagine how much work twins must be.'

And she was right; having twins is bloody hard. My insecurity was misplaced, because the fact of the matter is that I was being a mum. I wasn't just getting up in the night, I was caring for our two boys every day. I took them to mother and baby groups; I put them in the double buggy and walked along the seafront to Hove and back in the freezing cold just so they would sleep. I comforted them if they cried and distracted them if they were bored. I was being A MUM and guess what, I wasn't completely terrible at it.

So, what the hell was my problem?

I've always suffered from imposter syndrome. I guess with hindsight, I would say that I've had it most of my life. I can remember being at school and not feeling like I understood other girls my age. I pretended to be interested in boys; I deliberately made jokes to deflect my lack of knowledge, or passion for make-up or girls' magazines. I preferred playing any sport, reading or just hanging out with my brothers. I was an outsider pretending to fit in.

You would think after coming out of the closet I would have reconciled that notion and moved on, but that feeling has stayed with me most of my life. Even as a stand-up comedian, which is a career created for odd bods and outsiders, I have always felt like an imposter. For a long time, I expected to be told that I was in the wrong job; that I wasn't good enough; that I didn't deserve to be there.

I'm sure if I'd invested in any kind of therapy for more than two sessions, I could easily trace the root of my insecurity, but I don't like talking about my feelings, having feelings or acknowledging feelings – unless that feeling is raging anger, in which I can wallow for days/months/years. I did try therapy for a short time but I developed such an overwhelming crush on my therapist that I stopped going. Yeah, I'm that person: 'Oh this seems tricky, I'll give it a miss.'

Suffice to say, it has taken me ten or fifteen years longer than most people to reach my current level of emotional maturity, and I'm perfectly happy with that, OK? There's absolutely no baggage to offload here: none at all. Besides, if I start scratching at that scab GOD KNOWS what we might find underneath. Better to leave it festering under there until the day I die. It's the healthiest way to live your life.

So, if I sometimes sound defensive, it's because I am. I am defensive about my role as the 'other mum' and I am defensive about the fact that I have to explain myself to every new person I meet and, yes, I can be defensive when people ask perfectly reasonable questions because they're annoying. And here's a little heads up, if you do meet an 'other' parent and they're not forthcoming with any further information that's not a cue for you to bombard them with questions.

If you're not sure how gays can have kids, then google it.

Unwanted opinions, alas, seem to be simply part and parcel of having children. It's not the sole domain of 'other mums' by any means. One way or another ALL mums seem to have to suck it up.

People can't help but judge mums. I have a friend who doesn't even have kids who had the cheek to say to me:

'Jen, don't you think it's terrible when you see mums with their babies but they're not even looking at their babies, they're looking at their phones?'

'I tell you what, mate, when you have a kid, why don't you Velcro it to your face and then you can look at it all day every day!'

I don't think it's terrible, I think it's normal. If you've spent the day with a blob that has essentially done nothing but cry, gurgle, shit, puke, piss and sleep all day, you're allowed a cheeky look on Facebook. I have spent a lot of time with my two boys, bored out of my actual mind. If you see a mum looking at her phone it's because it's a lifeline to a world away from her baby.

I was guilty of being equally judgey myself in the past. I used to look at my friends with kids and think, 'Come on, mate! Make an effort, will you? How hard is it to play with your daughter for an hour?' (I am very glad I didn't voice that particular unasked-for opinion out loud.) Even now I think I would do anything for my boys: throw myself in front of a bus; give them all of my major organs; walk across a desert to save them but I WILL NOT PLAY LEGO SUPER-HEROES FOR THE TENTH TIME TODAY![1]

The fact is you'll never be invited to a bigger and more competitive contest (that you didn't knowingly enter) than being a mum. (I'd say 'being a parent', but dads are given WAY MORE slack.) Mums get judged a lot more harshly than dads. Dads are congratulated for just turning up. You just see a guy out and about with his kids, and hearts melt. See that same bloke staring at his phone while his two-year-old exits the play-ground and is stopped just before he/she runs out into the middle of oncoming traffic, and the surrounding mums will sigh and roll their eyes, 'Blokes, eh? What are they like?'

Find yourself in a supermarket as the mum with two toddlers screaming because *you* won't let them eat a whole family-size bag of Haribo, however, and you'll find that the empathy vacuum is all encompassing.

Equally, online parenting forums and mums' social media sites – the very places you turn to for reassur-ance that you're not a terrible parent – are a hotbed of passive aggression, strident opinion and unrelenting dogma. You'll find little comfort there, I can assure you. There's always one mum who has read too many

---

[1] I think this is perfectly reasonable.

baby books and managed to remember only the most extreme and controversial theories on paediatric nutrition and medicine:

'SUGAR IS POISON!'

'MMR VACCINATIONS ARE CAUSING TSUNAMIS IN SOUTH INDIA!'

'EXPOSING CHILDREN TO DAIRY PRODUCTS CAN MAKE THEM BALD!'

OK, so I'm exaggerating a little, but shouldn't we all chill out a bit? Also, let's not forget that this kind of opinionated claptrap is almost exclusively the domain of first-time mums. You're not going to see a mum with two or three kids panicking about sugar intake because they allow their kids the occasional chocolate biscuit.

I can remember going to my friend's house after the birth of her third kid. Her boys were running around like feral monkeys as we tried to navigate a route past them to the kitchen. We were about to have a glass of wine, when I saw signs of life-threatening activity by the television set.

'Quick – I think your Theo's got his finger stuck in the plug socket ...' I yelped, and made a grab for the middle boy.

'Leave him, we've got another two. Open that Pinot Grigio for me, will you ...'

Maybe it's easier with one, I don't know. I have seen couples meandering along Brighton seafront with one baby in tow looking pretty serene. Or at least, that's how they looked to me. When the boys were smaller, I always seemed to have a face on me that suggested I'd given up. I know this because of the number of times people said the following to me:

'Cheer up love, it might never happen!'

Well it has happened mate, just now. I was fine walking down the street, minding my own business with my usual resting bitch face, and then you ruined my inner chi with your inane and frankly IRRITAT-ING comment! And how do you know it *hasn't* happened? Hmm? How do *you know* that my dog hasn't died, I failed my driving test for the fifth time, or I haven't just lost the string on my tampon? SO WHY DON'T YOU BOG OFF, YOU MASSIVE PLANK!

If there's one thing worse, however, than an unin-vited opinion from someone who is in no position to judge, it's the gift of an unwanted opinion from a smug fellow parent. I reserved particular loathing for people who managed to get their babies to nap twice a day from the get-go.

'I'm just going to put Freya down for a nap.'

'Will she just sleep if you leave her like that?'

'She'll wriggle about a bit but eventually she'll go to sleep.'

'Oh … For how long?'

'Two or three hours. Sometimes I have to wake her up!'

WHAT THE ACTUAL WHAT? YOU CAN LEAVE YOUR BABY IN A COT AND SHE JUST GOES TO SLEEP?

So many smug parents out there are swanning about with their ONE BABY who sleeps, thinking that they've nailed parenting. I'm here to tell you all that they are completely deluded. It's got NOTHING to do with their brilliant parenting skills. They've just got lucky, that's all! Have another baby, mate, and let's see how you get on, because I can guarantee you won't be so lucky second time round!

There, I've said it.

Mums who have a baby who sleeps seem to actually believe it's because of something they're doing right, and aren't they pleased with themselves. They're very generous with their advice too.

'Have you tried waiting until he's nearly asleep but not quite asleep before putting him in his cot ... ?'

'Have you tried opening the window in his room? I find that the fresh air and the sound of the birds and rustling leaves really helps my son go to sleep ... '

'Have you tried putting a vacuum cleaner close to your baby's ear? I find that the white noise is a very effective way of calming your baby ...'

'Have you tried taking your unwanted advice and shoving it up your gluten-free chuff?'

Come on, WE HAVE ALL THOUGHT IT.

The fact is that some babies sleep and some babies don't sleep. You might have a baby who is up yowling every hour for the first nine months and then, all of a sudden, it miraculously starts to sleep through the whole night. And vice versa. Or, if you've hit the mother-of-all-crap-pots like we did, you might have two babies WHO DON'T SLEEP BECAUSE THEY HAVE BEEN BORN TO TEST YOUR PHYSICAL AND MENTAL HEALTH AND SEE HOW FAR THEY CAN PUSH YOU BEFORE YOU BREAK DOWN IN YOUR LOCAL CO-OP, TRYING TO FIGURE OUT THE DIFFERENCE BETWEEN GREEK YOGHURT AND GREEK-TASTING YOGHURT.[2]

If, however and unfortunately, that is the case, then the last thing you want to hear from anyone is:

'I'm so sorry to hear your boys aren't sleeping. My Noah here, he's slept through the night since birth. I think it's something to do with the energy you give your children. I really believe that if you give your children positive energy, they really feed off that energy and internalise it and it helps them ...'

Seriously: do one, love. It's got nothing to do with your bloody energy – if you want to know why your kid is sleeping it's probably because you've bored them

---

[2] Controversial I know, but I'm going to say that Greek yoghurt is infinitely better.

to death with your tedious Kirsty-Allsop-worshipping bullshit!

You can't say that, though; you have to pretend to give a shit about how they make their own almond milk and the colour of their husband's aura since he started hot yoga.

But even worse than the mums with napping babies are the mums whose kids have grown up. They know it all, those mums. They've been there, done it all, brilliantly no doubt, and feel compelled to give you the benefit of their unsolicited advice.

'I think he's just crying because he's tired.'

'Oh, you do, do you? And how would you know? Have you been with my baby all day? WERE YOU HERE FIVE MINUTES AGO WHEN HE WOKE UP FROM A TWO-HOUR NAP? I DIDN'T THINK SO, SO JOG ON, LOVE!'

But when it comes to advice that is both unwanted and frankly off-beam, that particular crown has to go to the grandparents. When it comes to how I parent my boys, my mum has plenty of opinions. All grandparents do, even the ones who pretend they don't.

'I don't want to interfere … but don't you think you ought to …'

They can't help themselves.

Chloe's mum is the same, except her approach is different. When we visit her house, her thoughts/opinions/ideas will be broached in the form of a newspaper or magazine article, carefully cut out and left on a chest of drawers by Chloe's bed.

When the boys were babies, of course there were times when Chlo and I would call our respective mums to mine them for advice. We assumed that all mothers, old and new, were a fount of knowledge that you could tap into with any questions or anxieties.

We couldn't have been more wrong: for some people, parenthood can cause amnesia, it seems. For every hundred know-it-all experienced mums out there just waiting to pounce with their unsolicited advice, there is an equivalent number who no longer have any idea what they were doing with their child six months ago, let alone ten years ago. Ask a member of these memory-loss parents for some much-needed advice, and you'll get the same response:

'God knows. I think we fed them ... I can't really remember.'

Thanks, I'll take that on board.

The boys' grandparents, that is mine and Chloe's parents, are the worst. Not only have they no recollection of what they were doing when they were *our* parents, they have also managed to misremember every memory they *have* retained, recasting their version of family history through heavily rose-tinted spectacles.

'We never had any problem. You and your brothers slept through the night from birth.'

Or:

'We never had you in bed with us.'

'So, how did you get any sleep?'

'We closed your bedroom door.'

Or:

'Are you not supposed to feed a baby every two hours for the first few weeks?'

'Oh, we didn't do that in the Seventies.'

Or:

'We just didn't breastfeed babies after six months.'

'Well, Mum, we are because it's easier to do that than faff around with bottles.'

'I NEVER used a bottle, you went from the boob to a cup.'

'I was drinking from a cup at six months?'

'You were very advanced.'

Not helpful.

Then there was one of the most divisive of all parenting dilemmas: dummies. Everyone has an opinion on that hot potato.

Five months in, when the little one was crying all the time, all day, all night long, Chloe's mum suggested we try a dummy. My mum said we had to do what we had to in order to comfort him.

Before the babies were born, we had our own pretty strong stance on the subject: Chlo and I were adamant that we wouldn't use dummies. We knew that for sure: there was no way José that we were going to rely on a piece of plastic to pacify our children. We would be such amazing parents, they wouldn't need one because we would teach them to comfort themselves.

But faced with the choice in real life, with a baby who screamed twenty-four-seven, what did we decide to do? We immediately ditched our earlier values of 'no dummies' and promptly went out to the nearest chemist's shop and bought six of them.

The big one immediately took to his dummy. We were so delighted, we even took a photo of it! (Of course, we did.) I can remember Chlo and I high-fiving each other at this achievement, we felt so smug. The little one, however, wasn't having it: every time we tried to put it in his mouth, he screamed and spat it out.

But at least the bigger one was using his. That was something, right?

It would have been ... but the very next day, he spat it out and refused to let it anywhere near his face again.

WHAT IS WRONG WITH THESE PEOPLE? MAKE A DECISION AND BLOODY STICK TO IT, WILL YOU?

Not to be deterred, Chloe and I persevered. We had a goal and that goal was five minutes of peace and quiet. And let's not forget we'd invested in a pack of six.

Eventually, the little one succumbed and soon after, so did the bigger one. Now if they cried, we had something we could stuff in their gobs that immediately comforted them. It was a revelation! We were so proud of ourselves! WELL DONE US!

As I said above, dummies, however, can split a room. Get on Mumsnet, if you dare, and, blimey, you will see that a lot of people have *very* strong views about dummies:

'I would never let my baby use a pacifier. I've heard they can change the shape of your child's mouth so they only speak with a Russian accent!'

'Dummies are unhygienic and you can't recycle them, in fact they are probably responsible for making up six per cent of all landfills globally!'

'Parents who let their babies use dummies are the same kind of people who think it's OK for a two-year-old to watch television, drink fruit juice and wear mixed-cotton socks!'

Yeah, that's us.

If you haven't got a kid and you are planning to have one, I bet you're reading this thinking:

'I will never be like that beige lezza. I will be a calm, knowing, connected, ever-patient, loving, intuitive, resilient Earth Mother. I will never be that haggard-looking woman, staggering through a kid's playground with some kind of weird white stain on her front, staring at her phone as her children chew on grass that a dog may or may not have urinated on seconds earlier.'

Yeah, well, the proof is in the pudding, love, so reserve your judgement and let's regroup when you're six months into chronic sleep deprivation, shit, vom and no adult conversation.

Maybe I just have a problem with advice, whatever the source. I'm not a fan of advice books, self-help books, books by experts, or those 'How to Do Anything ...' books, if I'm honest, although by now you no doubt have formed the opinion that I would probably benefit from reading a few. I'm just not good with instruction; I have spent my life winging everything and it seems to have worked for me. (Again, I say that as someone who has taken twice as long to get anywhere in their career as anyone else, but I'm going to dogmatically stand by my decision, mainly because it's too late to do anything about it.)

I dipped into the few mother and baby books that Chloe had collected, but that ended up confusing me because they were all either too earnest, or too dictatorial. So, I mostly ignored the books, and to be fair, so did Chloe, preferring to google the crap out of every question we had. Google is our third parent. Any question we ever had, we googled it, because what you want as a parent is six or seven conflicting and contradictory answers to every question you have.

That's the thing about looking after a baby: by the time the boys were about a year old, the main lesson we'd learned is that most of the time you're faking it and just hoping no one else notices that you have no idea what you're doing. It was beginning to dawn on us that nobody had all the answers, or the definitive answers, or any answers at all.

In case you are still wondering or concerned about our sleep problems, our boys did nap eventually and I can tell you that it's not because we tried this or tried that. I can't give you any advice on that front, even if you begged me for it, because, honestly, I think they just started napping because they were knackered and they wanted to.

Whether it be sleeping, weaning or potty-training, they ended up getting the hang of it, eventually, by themselves and no doubt in spite of our best efforts. Everything they've done, they've done it because *they* wanted to do it. As a parent, all you can do is try not to lose your mind in the interim.

There you have it: that's my piece of unwanted, unsolicited advice.

You're welcome.

13

The New Me

Suddenly, the boys were zooming everywhere. I hadn't really anticipated how much more work it would be once they were no longer static. The bigger one had been toddling about without any help since he was ten months old. The little one caught up shortly after their first birthday, but was still so small he looked like a walking six-month-old.

Even at just a year old, they were already both so different. The big one has olive skin and blue eyes, and is absolutely gorgeous. The little one has fairer skin and hazel eyes, a cheeky face and winning smile. The big one is strong, singular, determined, but also so very sensitive and doesn't like being held by anyone he doesn't know. The little one is a tiny charisma bomb who knows exactly how to manipulate us. He knows that he makes us laugh and loves the attention.

I know that I love them more than I'd loved anyone or anything in my life. In many ways, they are the best thing that has ever happened to me and in other ways …

They have ruined my life.

OK, not ruined, just irrevocably changed.

Possibly, because I was nearly forty when I became a parent, it took a while for me to reconcile the fact that my old life was gone.

Over the first year of parenthood, I slowly transformed into a new person. The demands the babies made on my time made every spare second I had more precious, so that by the time they were one year old, I was amazed to find how much I was managing to get done. Now that I had no time to speak of, I had become infinitely more productive.

What the hell had I been doing, I wondered, with all that free time before they born? Before the boys arrived, I could go for days and days with nothing to do until my gig in the evening. I know I was writing, but I was still writing now. So, what had I been doing between the writing? How many trips to the fridge and cups of tea must I have made to squander all that time?

For those of you who don't have children, if you think you're using your time effectively, I can tell you now that you're not. Have a baby, seriously, just one (not twins – that's madness) and you will get shit done. When you have a two-hour window to do your accounts, send a few invoices, make dinner, do the washing-up and put the bins out, you tick everything off your list.

Pre kids, I could go for days in my flat lounging about in my pyjamas, ignoring the smell of the over-flowing bin and staring out of the window as Chloe complained that she'd found yet another box of my receipts under the sink. Post kids, I became an efficiency ninja. Yes, there are still boxes of receipts I haven't looked at in months, but they're now sitting on a shelf in the study. I know, it's like I'm a grown-up.

The changes went deeper than getting to grips with my tax returns, though. When my children were born, I was catapulted out of my narcissistic cocoon and into a world where I was no longer the centre of my own uni-verse; a world (or do I mean universe, or maybe a gal-axy?) where my egotistic concerns were so peripheral I felt like the planet Pluto[1] ... what I'm trying to say is that when it came to being prioritised in the family, I was the furthest away from the heat of the sun.

---

[1] Once considered the ninth and most distant planet from the sun and now the largest known dwarf planet in the solar system. Nice to have these facts, isn't it? You're welcome.

(I'm not sure if this analogy works either, but I'm sticking with it.)

It has been good for me. It has been life-changing and it has made me a better person. There, I've said it. If I'd heard someone utter those words before my own children were born, they would have made my eyes roll right to the back of my head. Now that I'm a changed person, though, I even find myself uttering sentences that start with the words, 'As a mother ...', as if I'm auditioning for a part in a badly conceived musical sponsored by the *Daily Mail*.

I'm not saying I stopped being self-involved over-night: I'm just saying my needs and wants had to be shelved because we had two baby boys who took priority.

Up until their birth, I had always defined myself by my job: I am a comedian. Being a comedian was what fed my ego, gave me a sense of self and a purpose or point to my day.

While most normal people are not defined solely by their job or career, stand-up comedians, on the contrary, are self-involved spoons, often pathologically consumed by insecurity and self-loathing, and unable to function without the approbation and adoration of strangers. You can imagine how unhealthy it is to be constantly indulging in that level of solipsism on a daily basis. We're not right in the head. What's more, with the advent of social media, needy dickheads like me have even more opportunities to feed our hunger for affirmation through every retweet, Instagram like and Facebook share. It's utterly gross.

I know, I hate me too.

My career was moving at such a glacial pace it was hard to know if I was making any progress. I felt stunted and trapped, that I was never going to be able to move to the next level, whatever that was. I was constantly living somewhere in the future. Life would be better if I got that gig, or made more money, or managed to write a critically acclaimed stand-up show, or I got on TV, or I wrote a sitcom script, or signed with a new agent, or I took acting classes ... I could feel myself panicking and began to strangle my career by putting myself under so much pressure at every single gig. I didn't even enjoy performing any more.

I could feel myself becoming resentful of others' successes (something I've always hated in others and vowed never to indulge in myself). I had become creatively constipated, hating the material I was producing but unable to articulate what I really wanted to say and make it funny. In short, I was horrific company.

Chloe had to put up with a lot. No one wants to live with a frustrated and depressed creative, they are the WORST PEOPLE IN THE WORLD. You can't make them feel better, you can't really help them because they don't want help and if you even think about offering any advice, then think again:

'Jen, have you thought about doing something else?'

'I don't want to do anything else.'

'It's just that I don't think stand-up comedy is making you happy ...'

'I AM HAPPY! I'VE NEVER BEEN HAPPIER! THIS IS ME BEING HAPPY, OK?'

God. Imagine that for eight years?

My career *is* important to me; I didn't want to stop doing it, however unhappy or mad it was making me. I have given up having a social life, seeing friends, going on holiday. I have missed weddings, birthdays, weekends away because I didn't want to give up the opportunity of work. I had spent most of my twenties and all of my thirties on the road trying get to a gig, staying in shitty hotels, eating crap food at service stations, and almost exclusively hanging out with other comedians. I am a dogmatic, fairly confrontational, overly emotive, dissatisfied human who is firmly stuck in her ways. The last thing I was expecting to change was me.

Anyone who knows me will know that the one thing I've always avoided is self-improvement. I abandoned therapy before I'd properly embarked on it, I've never read a self-help book, gone on a course, or explored my inner chi. I don't like talking about my feelings or exploring the reasons why my behaviour might be self-destructive.

I think most things that I might benefit from are a load of old bollocks. It's my default setting. I am, in many ways, a complete idiot. Even with this self-awareness I still refuse to do anything about it. My cup is half empty, please don't try and fill it, OK?

Before we had the children, I never really understood what mindfulness was either. When I listened to those meditation CDs that Chloe had, I thought that was a load of old bollocks too.

BUT, once the boys arrived, I found myself practising my own version of mindfulness – another sentence I'd never have imagined coming out of my mouth – and that is being a parent to twin boys. There were days, weeks, months where both Chloe and I were only just about functioning, yet it was because of this that I was forced to live in the present.

I had to give them all of my attention, my focus, my love, and so could no longer sustain that level of self-indulgence, self-loathing, self-anything that had consumed and paralysed me before. I couldn't think about anything other than surviving this time, this day, this moment – therefore I somehow couldn't obsess, or indulge in the endless negative rumination about my career.

Once I had unconsciously taken all the pressure off myself, things started to resolve themselves with my work. The gigs went better, I started to enjoy myself again. I don't think it's an exaggeration to say that the children had a huge impact on my mental health, for the better.

A year into being a parent, and I couldn't remember what my life had been like before. Their very presence had become all-consuming and I finally fully accepted that *this* is my life now. I am living day to day, not just with them, but with my work, in my relationship, in my life.

Which is why, in so many ways, I'm grateful for my children. They have changed my perspective, my values, even my self-worth. They have given me a focus I had no idea I needed. I am a different person thanks to their presence and the relentless pressures of loving and caring for them.

For the first time in a very long time, I feel quite free.

If that sounds too good to be true, that's because it is. There were of course the downsides. While I was having my life changed irrevocably, our social life had ground to a halt and it has pretty much stayed that way since. The closest I get to partying is downing a drink in the green room after a gig, which I rarely do because I usually just want to go home and go to sleep.

The 'new me' thinks socialising is overrated and, anyway, I am generally pleased that my lack of fun has kept pace with Chloe's. Not long after I'd got back from the Edinburgh Festival, when Chloe was about nine months pregnant, I can clearly remember talking to a mate at a mutual friend's wedding. He and his wife had just had a baby girl. He was enthusing positively about his daughter and how great things were.

'Honestly, Jen, people will tell you that your life changes when you have a kid, but it doesn't have to. It's a state of mind, mate!'

A state of mind? He's right! We weren't going to be like those other loser parents who had their lives turned upside down by children. We were going to be that couple that carried on living our lives as before. Babies would have to fit in with us, not the other way around!

If I had taken the time and looked a bit closer, I might have noticed his wife breastfeeding their daughter in the corner of the room as he chugged down a bottle of lager. I might have seen the dark circles around her eyes from being up all night, feeding and changing her daughter, I might have noticed that she was responsible for 90 per cent of the childcare – and then I might have given my mate a slap.

It's easy to think your life hasn't really changed when YOUR LIFE hasn't really changed. Going to work, drinks out with mates, work trips abroad and then getting home just as your baby goes to bed. Not getting up in the night because YOU have to go to work so can't be expected to get up. Yeah, I can see how you'd get that impression. Probably doesn't feel the same for your partner stuck at home with a baby, a chronic case of sleep deprivation and conversation that revolves almost entirely around breast-feeding, when you should start potty-training and *Peppa* fucking *Pig*.

Life as a couple just isn't the same after kids. Navigating coupledom with toddlers required a whole new toolkit of hippie mantras. Listening, trust, non-judgement, you name it. Lucky the kids had brought out this new renaissance me or I don't know how Chloe would have handled it.

14

Fun Tax

Chloe and I had some passive-aggressive issues to resolve during the kids' first year. And it'll come as no surprise to hear they mainly revolved around sleep.

When it is 4am and the kids are crying and you've been up three times already, you can't help but resent the fact that your partner is still asleep; even if you know that they deserve some shut-eye, there is still a part of you that begrudges every extra minute they have in bed.

The plus side of getting up for the early shift, of course, is that you can throw it back in your partner's face later in the day as you inevitably engage in the biggest competition of your relationship: 'Who has had the least sleep?'

The winner is of course the person who can convince the other that they are the most tired. To be honest, there are no real winners in this so-called competition but that doesn't seem to stop anyone from trying.

'I'm exhausted!'

'I only got three hours' sleep last night.'

'I feel like I've had three hours' sleep all week.'

'You had a lie-in yesterday.'

'I didn't get to bed until two a.m.!'

'I didn't get to bed till one a.m. and I was up at five a.m.'

'Well, I got less sleep because I got up three times in the night!'

'I literally never sleep! Ever. I work twenty-three hours a day and I survive solely on caffeine and did I mention that I double-breastfed our children for six months?'

'I don't think you appreciate how hard it is to stand up in front of a room full of people for twenty minutes! OK FINE! ... You win.'

Obviously, I'm paraphrasing. I can't repeat a lot of what was actually said – or so my editor has told me.

There have been times when I have woken in the night to hear one or both of my boys crying and looked at my girlfriend sleeping soundly without a care in the world and thought:

'She must be exhausted, she got up early this morning and she's worked really hard all day ... but I did get up twice already so, strictly speaking, it's her turn, so she needs to wake up now … What the hell is wrong with her? Why can't she hear them screaming? Is she pretending to be asleep? I bet she's pretending to be asleep! Well, it looks like MUGGINS HAS TO GET UP AGAIN!'

I get up. I tend to my children, I cuddle them, re-assure them and sometimes even rock them to sleep, all the while making a passive-aggressive mental note of 'what a perfect parent I am', which I will later throw back in my girlfriend's face at the mere infer-ence that she might be tired.

I know what you're thinking: how petty *are you*, Brister? I'm petty. I'm very petty. I'm the Tom Petty of petty. Why? Because I'm KNACKERED!

Obsessions are never healthy and they make you boring. People who are obsessed with anyone or any-thing are generally tedious. Just ask the partner of any Olympian. Sure, they're proud of their achievements but somewhere in the back of their mind they're thinking, 'I love that Jean is so good at hurdling, but Christ she's dull.' For anyone reading this who is an Olympian I'm sorry you had to find out here, but just know we're all thinking it.

Deep down, I knew I had to suck it up and get up with the kids. I also knew I needed to give Chloe the respect she deserved for playing her part. So, during the first year, I did relationship therapy my way. In the form of some heavy-duty self-medication. My poison? Red wine. I know, it doesn't sound too healthy, it wasn't, but let me tell you it was honestly the only thing I had to look forward to.

I would drink most nights, not get hammered, but just a glass of wine, maybe two, sometimes three, in front of the telly. Just to soften the edges, make the day seem a little better. I craved wine and by 7pm I would be cooking dinner with a bottle on the go. When I wasn't working, it was the one thing that felt like a luxury, or a reward, or a sedative. Whatever the reason, I wanted wine and I was going to have wine and nothing was going to get in the way of me indulging in my nightly tipple.

Except maybe a bottle opener.

I'm not saying that in that first year of parenthood I had a drinking problem, but one night, after breaking our only corkscrew, I left my house, walked into two different shops and knocked on several strangers' doors to see if someone, anyone, could open my bottle of wine.

Can you believe that no one had a corkscrew? Me neither. Perhaps the sight of a deranged woman standing on their doorstep clutching a bottle of wine with a broken cork (with teeth marks) in it, was enough for them to decide they 'didn't have one'.

If you google how to open a bottle of wine without a corkscrew you will find some pretty innovative suggestions and I can tell you, in all sincerity, that I tried most of them.

Place your bottle inside a shoe and hit the shoe against a wall – Check.

Twist it out with a key or screwdriver – Check.

Pull the cork out with string – Check.

Wrap a towel round the bottom of the bottle and bang it against the floor – Check.

Pump your bottle with a bicycle pump until the cork pops out – I'm not that desperate.[1]

I could go on, but I think you get the idea.

It's hard to maintain any dignity when you're wandering around your house with a bottle of wine in a shoe, banging it against random walls and swearing. Chloe didn't seem to understand the urgency or desperation of the situation.

'Jen, if you just wait 'til tomorrow morning, you can just buy a corkscrew!'

'I can't wait until tomorrow! I need a drink NOW!'

With hindsight it seems bloody ridiculous to be so focused on guzzling the one thing that would make getting out of bed in the middle of the night / early morning harder. But my logic was that I already felt like I had a hangover, so I might as well enjoy a bloody drink.

---

[1] I am, I just didn't have a bicycle pump.

I'm pretty sure Chlo lost a bit of respect for me in that moment: the jury's out as to whether I ever managed to claw any of it back.

I guess it's OK to admit that I struggle at being 'a parent'. I can't be alone in feeling overwhelmed by the sheer relentlessness of it all. There doesn't appear to be any quality 'downtime'. Sure, we get our evenings 'off', but by 7pm I'm catatonic. I can barely string a sentence together, let alone 'make the most of my evening'. And Radio 4 can bog off; no one wants to hear famous authorly types bang on about how inspired and creative they became once they had children:

'I wrote my first three books in under a year after my first child was born.'

Good for you, love, I've just written a shopping list and I'm going for a lie down.

I know what you're thinking, 'Hang on, you've written this book!' Yes, I have, four years later, not when I was up to my eyeballs in piss, shit and tears. I can sit here and write because they're not here, they're at nursery.

Anyway, somehow my body was able to cope with the daily abuse, probably because my alcohol intake was steady, rather than bingeing. So, I never had a hangover. Of course, I felt dreadful, but I always felt dreadful, because I was only getting four hours of sleep a night on average, if that. The booze probably wasn't helping, but by the same token, I don't think it was making me feel that much worse, and at the time I was willing to take it if it gave me the carrot I needed at the end of a very long day.

It won't surprise you to hear that, unlike me, Chloe wasn't really drinking much, if at all, during this whole time. I think she may have had the occasional glass of wine, but rarely and one glass was nearly always enough. Needless to say, her body was therefore not hardened to booze, which she lived to regret ...

Just after the boys turned one, we had our first night out with the mums from our NCT group. Since the boys' birth Chloe and I had only had one meal out together, so a night out felt like a bit of a novelty. A mate came to babysit; she had bravely/stupidly donated her time as a gift to us and we were cashing it in. Not having children, she had naively told us to, 'Stay out as long as we wanted!'

We guiltily, if very quickly, gave her instructions as we backed out the door.

It wasn't going to be a BIG night, just a few mates having a couple of glasses of wine in a bar in Brighton. I could tell Chloe was a bit giddy because she'd already told me how excited she was to be out of the house about thirty-four times in the first ten minutes of leaving the house;

'I can't bloody wait to have a drink!'

'It'll be nice to catch up with everyone and see how they're ...'

'I'm not going to drink too much. Just a couple of glasses of wine.'

'Yeah, you don't want to get hammered.'

'It's so nice to be out! WE CAN HAVE A DRINK TOGETHER!'

It's not like Chloe hadn't been out at all since the boys were born, in fact when they were less than three months old, she had attended a Christmas party that she and her business partner organise every year for a group of freelancer mates. She hadn't had a drop to drink and returned home with a soaking wet top and swollen and painful breasts like boulders. It turns out she'd spent most of the night in the ladies' toilets with a breast pump trying to alleviate the pressure on her bursting tits.

Fun times.

Tonight, however, we could walk into town, have a civilised night out with like-minded pals, and meander home.

What could possibly go wrong?

On arriving at the bar, we found our gang and grabbed a couple of tables. Chloe and I were quickly separated as she sat at one table and I found myself at another.

Bottles of Prosecco were bought, drinks were poured and we all settled down for a proper catch-up.

It just happened that my trio of mums weren't really drinking because they either had work the next day, or their babies didn't take to bottles and so they were still breastfeeding. Whatever the reason, it meant that our table was taking it very slow booze-wise. There's no doubt that I probably had more than everyone else, but by my standards, I was taking it easy.

Chloe's table, on the other hand, was being managed by let's call her Lucy. We all like Lucy but she has way more stamina, youth and energy than the rest of us put together. Once the Prosecco was done, red wine was ordered and when that bottle was finished more red wine was ordered, followed by another bottle, and ANOTHER bottle ...

Every time I looked over to see how Chloe was doing, she looked like she was having the time of her life. There was wild gesticulating and raucous laughter. As my table began to wind down and leave, I found myself joining the 'other table' and quickly realised that booze-wise, I was lagging behind.

Call it instinct, but I didn't go hell for leather that night and by 11pm, I'd had enough anyway. It was only when we all got up to leave that I realised just how hammered Chloe was.

Fortunately for me, Chlo is a great drunk. By that, I mean she is a lot of fun. She doesn't get belligerent or angry, she doesn't try to start a fight, or shout abuse at men for no reason. What I'm saying is, she's not me.

What she does do, is giggle a lot, talk ever so slightly louder than usual, and hang off your arm like a monkey.

Staggering back home, I had to hold Chloe up for most of the way. By the time we got home her upbeat and ebullient behaviour had ebbed considerably:

'I feel sick.'

'Don't worry, love, we're nearly home. You'll feel better after a glass of water.'

It must have been close to midnight by the time we got home and, as I fished around for my keys, I could hear Chloe groaning,

'Euuuurgh ... ! I feel terrible. Hurry up!'

Falling through our front door, Chloe took three steps into the living room, fell to her knees and promptly threw up on to our rug again and again and again.

'Good night, was it?'

'Yeah ... you could say that.'

You don't need to know the ins and outs of the state of the rug, or how long it took to clean. You just need to know that we no longer have it.

I've never seen Chloe as sick as that before or since. Even after her gargantuan expulsion, she managed to throw up again in our bed, then in a bucket and finally in the toilet.

The beauty of babies is that they don't know or care if you're hungover, or ill, or knackered, they're just going to do what they always do, which for our two meant waking up every couple of hours before I had to admit defeat and take them both downstairs at 6am.

The lesson we learned that day is that you can have fun, of course you can, but as fellow comedian and mate Kerry Godliman warned, there is always a 'fun tax' to pay and for us that tax is a hangover plus two babies.

That, dear Reader, is the worst possible combination because it doesn't matter how much fun you think you're having at 2am dancing to Rihanna and slamming your fifth flaming sambuca into your face, nothing says regret more than finding yourself lying prone on your living room floor sweating into a rug (that you probably threw up on the night before), as your sons use your limp and lifeless body as a trampoline.

15

Two Birds and Two Babies

I had always thought that, when I had kids, I would want to be with them all the time, I would never send them to nursery! At twelve months on the dot we sent them to nursery.

I think you might be seeing a pattern here: that is, we're nothing if not pragmatic.

It's all very well wanting to be that perfect mum but the fact is, most of us have to work. There is no question that at this point, when the boys were a year old, Chlo was the main breadwinner, even though both of us had been working the entire time. We had been juggling the childcare between us for a year, and even though I was a changed woman – as I've said, I'd become a master of efficiency and was getting more done in my brief periods of respite than ever before – it had become impossible to do both.

Even after twelve months I was really keen to spend as much time as I could with the boys, but I was still working at night; I knew I couldn't be a full-time parent and a stand-up comedian. Often, I was away at weekends and then as soon as I got back, I'd have the children all week and then I'd be working again from Thursday through to Sunday. It was killing me. I was also aware that I was treading water and I desperately needed to start building some momentum if I was going to make anything of my career.

I just needed some time.

We had visited a few nurseries nearby and after choosing one we decided that we'd put the boys in for a day twice a week. It doesn't sound much, but those extra two days meant I could finally get some extended periods of work.

The nursery we chose was near our house, we liked the people who worked there and we had a couple of NCT pals who were also sending their kid there. It felt like a good fit.

Despite all of that, every time we had to leave our boys at the nursery, Chlo and I felt like the WORST people on the planet. We'd try to drop them off and leave quickly so as not to delay and prolong the trauma, but as we tried to get out the door, watching them scream their hearts out was like having our guts wrenched from our stomach.

I felt guilty all the time. Something didn't feel right about leaving them for ten hours when they were so little; both of us hated not having them around, particularly as neither of us had to go to work in an office. But equally we needed to make some money. We had talked about getting a nanny, not just because we liked the idea of having them at home for a bit longer, but also because we needed a bit more flexibility so I could start picking up work mid-week and Chlo could try to squeeze a full week's work into four days, and the nursery was about as accommodating as a plank of wood.

There's something weird about saying you have a nanny for your children. The whole idea felt weird; a bit like saying you love polo tournaments and skiing in Val d'Isère, you can't help sounding drenched in privilege and like a complete prick. It was the most middle-class thing we'd ever discussed and we'd tried hot yoga.

The flip side was that we'd get to pick the days we needed from week to week, which meant I could gig mid-week, plus the boys would still be at home. It was win-win. We started interviewing potential nannies. The kids lasted a month in nursery before we pulled them out. They couldn't have been happier and we both felt our guilt recede.

The boys loved their new nanny. Soraya was great with them. Confident, kind, affectionate but firm. We loved her as much as the kids did even if she was a vegan[1] who was obsessed with CrossFit.[2] I guess no one's perfect.

If you don't know what CrossFit is, it's basically circuit training with a group of people who like exercising with their tops off, comparing six packs and drinking protein shakes. Or at least that's what it sounds like. Personally, I'd rather let my one pack hang over my tracksuit bottoms as I lounge on the sofa watching crap TV.

That doesn't mean I don't want to be fit, of course I do. Sadly, I can barely get out of bed, so the idea of being shouted at to do ten more squats by some buff exercise-zealot in Lycra shorts doesn't really appeal. Besides, there's enough pressure to be a good parent; I can't be expected to look like a normal human being *and* keep on top of my fitness regime.

I have to say that I'm full of admiration[3] when I see mums running through the park, pushing their baby's buggy. I don't know about you but I often see those women and find myself thinking HOW IN GOD'S

---

[1] Yes, it's a cheap gag at the expense of vegans even though we know veganism is better for the environment etc. But I'm a dick, OK?

[2] We can all agree that Crossfit is a step too far.

[3] Horror.

GREEN EARTH DO THEY HAVE THE ENERGY TO DO THAT?

Since the birth of our sons, I have never woken up and thought, 'I know what I fancy: a run!'

Never, not once.

I'm not judging you if you are one of those women. I'm just asking, HOW? Seriously, HOW CAN YOU RUN? I can barely walk, sometimes I think I'll just get on my hands and knees and take the weight off my back. In fact, that's too much pressure on my knees, maybe I can just roll from the kitchen to the living room.

That's what I'd like to see; a park full of women with babies rolling around. No one ever gets up, no one even breaks into a sweat. We're all just lying on the ground, maybe having a little cry, maybe just taking a moment to assess all of our life choices, but mostly we're just rolling. I think we'd all go to that mother and baby group.

Still, you've got to do what you've got to do to stay sane, and if running in the park does that for you, then I salute you!

As I mentioned earlier, Chlo and I tried hot yoga, which on the face of it sounds very relaxing. I mean yoga, as we know, is all about stretching and meditating and is great for the body and mind. And heat, well I love a bit of heat! Put the two together and what have you got?

A great opportunity to pass out / throw up in public.

If you're thinking what a lightweight, then I challenge *you* to go to a hot yoga class. Yeah, just give it a try and then tell me how RELAXED and easy you found it, because it is neither of those things, in fact, it is the hardest work out I've ever had.

The classes we went to were almost entirely made up of women, with the one obligatory bloke in speedos with whom we avoided all eye contact. Every now and then, another cocky-looking fella would rock up, sometimes accompanied by his girlfriend, sometimes alone, and I confess I always enjoyed watching the inevitable pained look on his face as he struggled to maintain a single pose while simultaneously losing two litres of sweat.

If I learned nothing else from hot yoga it is this: women have more stamina than men. A gross generalisation with zero science to back it up? Perhaps. Nevertheless, it is a claim I will defend, dogmatically, to the day I die.

Obviously, we couldn't maintain our hot yoga attendance. Even though we had started to notice the benefits physically, and undoubtedly we both felt better mentally, the truth is that hot yoga is WAY TOO INTENSE for two women juggling twins *and* jobs. The sessions lasted ninety minutes, so by the time we got to the class, got changed, survived the class, showered the sweat off, got dried, dressed and walked back home, it had taken up the best part of a day.

We could have taken up some other kind of sport or exercise, I know that, but as work started to ramp up and I spent more time on the road, we had even less energy to do anything.

I'd like to say we got back into exercise recently – but that would be a big fat lie. Maybe when the kids are in school … Yeah, that's when we'll pick it back up again.

In the meantime, we'll be stuck to our sofa with a bar of Lindt chocolate and a bottle of wine.

Once Soraya was in our lives, I was starting to work more. With work came space for me, and a little distance from the day-in-day-out exhaustion of looking after the boys. It allowed me to take a step back and realise that despite the horrors of parenting, my boys are amazing. With that distance, time spent with them has become more precious and more enjoyable.

I can't help looking at them and thinking how beautiful and smart and funny they are. I spend quite a lot of my time recording and photographing their every waking move and have had to buy a 64G SD card because I quickly ran out of all device space; my phone is still basically just crammed full of photos and videos of them.

Chlo and I are paying for multiple clouds and drives and Dropboxes, just so that we can upload more photos and videos of our boys. Very quickly and seem-ingly without any self-awareness we have become *those* bloody parents: the very parents we swore we would never become.

I have to fight the urge to show people photos of my children all day, every day. I know that no one is inter-ested, I know this. Even when people ask to see a photo, I can tell they're asking out of politeness because in the time it's taken for me to retrieve my phone from my back pocket their eyes have glazed over. By this point, I could show them a stock photo of a St Bernard dog and they would make the requisite oohs and ahhs.

So, Reader, if you have a child or two or three or four (WHY WOULD YOU DO THAT TO YOUR-SELF?) don't talk about your kids to anyone who hasn't got kids, because they don't care, not even a lit-tle bit ...

'How's little Johnny?'

'He fell down the stairs on Thursday ...'

'Oh that's so sweet ... So are you going to Mike's wedding next month?'

I know it doesn't matter what I say – you, Reader, are thinking to yourself:

'Maybe *your* friends, Jen, but my friends love my kids.'

Trust me, they don't.

My friends love me and I love them and it's because I love them that I won't inflict my children on them is a lie that I have convinced myself of since my boys were born.

Remember that video I took of Twin Two being pulled out of Chloe's uterus? Yeah, well I made my friend Suzi watch it:

'You've got to see this!'

'Um ... What is it?'

'It's a video of the bigger one being born!'

'Mate, I really don't think I want to see ... Oh! Dear God ... .'

Not only did I make her watch it, I was crying while she watched it. Crying with joy, as I chose to ignore the fact that her face had visibly begun to crumble, the look of sheer incredulity and horror plain to see, as she watched my son being physically tugged out of a hole in Chloe's stomach.

Unbelievably, we're still friends.

I have always thought our boys were beautiful, from the second they were born. I didn't notice they were minute, had faces like raisins and basically resembled hairless baby moles. I've always thought they were perfect.

I was also convinced that they were super bright, supremely gifted and abnormally advanced for their age, even as I watched the bigger one stare blankly into the middle distance and the little one lick our kitchen radiator.

I'm probably going to be one of those irritating mums who tells their kids that they can do or be whatever they want – then watch as they go to school and have their dreams crushed as their ordinary, every-day limitations are publicly exposed.

Still, it's what my mum did for me, so I'm happy to pass that gift of motherhood on to my children.

That's the thing to remember as a parent, the upside of telling your children they can do anything is that they believe you. The downside, of course, is when they realise they can't be a doctor because they're average at maths and absolutely hopeless in all of the sciences and then stop believing anything their mum says from that moment on.

Yes, I am talking about me.

Self-belief is important and I am very grateful to my mum for always believing in me. There is no way I would be doing stand-up comedy without her dogged and unwavering support. She has always been, and con-tinues to be, my biggest fan. Although I think it's fair to say that she's ever so slightly over being one of the main topics (for topic: read butt) of my stand-up comedy.

'OK, can you talk about something else now? We know British people like laughing at my Spanish accent. Time to write something new.'

She's right, Brits like nothing more than laughing at a foreign accent, but she is also a very forthright, opinionated and dogmatic Spanish woman. A lot of my material has involved me standing in my mum's kitchen with a notepad and pen.

I'll give you an example: like the time I told my mum that Chloe and I were thinking of starting a family and my mum, who was washing up at the time, stopped what she was doing, turned to me and said:

'Oh, Yennifer, I do hope you know you cannot get pregnant with two fingers.'

People think I wrote that joke, I did not write that joke. It wasn't a joke, my mother actually said that to me.

Being a parent has made me rethink how I used to casually judge my mum. Now I dread to think what my boys might say about me when I'm older.

16

The Toddler Years

As soon as they were able to walk, the next chapter of my life as a parent began.

If you're not a parent, or your baby isn't up and about yet, you won't yet know much about this next phase in your life as a parent. Let me explain: basically once your child has mastered the basics of walking, unless you live in a stately home with its own extensive grounds and facilities, you will need to take your child out of your house, not only for your child's health and amusement, but for the sake of your sanity.

This means, therefore, that you will have to venture into pastures new, namely the playground / play group / petting farm / soft play / swimming pool / countryside / Nature.

Even if you are one of the rare few who likes the sound of all of the above, the early walking, toddler years are *interminable* and *tedious*. In fact, had I known how mind-bendingly boring this phase was going to be, I would have drunk a lot more.

Exhaustion and monotony were my enemy as a parent of toddler twins because, try as I might to stay in an ever-mindful state of consciousness, there were swathes of time when I was just not present. As a result, I doubtless missed out on my kids being funny/cute/engaging while I had been staring blankly at a wall, fantasising about a pint of wine, a hot bath and sleep. (These days I don't bother trying to romanticise being a parent because I know having a family is primarily hard work. Sure, you get heart-melting moments, we all do, but they are brief, because they are just 'MOMENTS'.)

At the start of the boys' toddler phase, I was still naive and, frankly, stupid enough to believe that I could and would enjoy every second of my time with my children and now that they were mobile and it was so much easier to get them out of the house, I couldn't wait to start exploring that big, beautiful world out there with them by my side – going to the beach, rampaging round the many local parks and playgrounds, exploring the woods, making mud pies.

Before our boys were born, Chlo and I had both looked forward to spending time with our children in the great outdoors. We had romanticised our out-door pursuits in every season. Playing with leaves in autumn, playing in the snow in the winter, running through shady glades of bluebells in springtime, and basking on long, lingering beach picnics in the summer.

How disappointing, therefore, that for the first few years of their lives our boys displayed an out-and-out aversion to sand, grass, water, snow and mud.

Sand was a no-no. (We discovered our sons' viru-lent dislike of this common beach surface while on our first attempt at a holiday in Dorset. I'll give you the further delights of that fun experiment in a moment.) I get that. I don't like it much either. What we weren't expecting is that they'd take a dislike to *all* of Nature.

If they weren't walking on pavements, tarmac, lino-leum, tiling, carpeting or floorboards, they'd lose it. The slightest speck of dirt on either of their hands would trigger a complete meltdown. Sometimes when we were out enjoying Nature in the park, they would just burst into tears for no apparent reason. They were sud-denly inconsolable with grief, so upset you were certain that something truly dreadful had happened, only to discover there was a leaf stuck to their Wellington boot.

I know they were only about one year old at the time, but time to grow up, Snowflake. It's a bloody leaf, for crying out loud!

The bigger one in particular couldn't handle grass. I mean GRASS, for heaven's sake. If he fell over, he would lie on his front, screaming, with his hands and feet off the ground like he was trying to skydive.

Once, when they were about twenty months I took them to a 'forest school' with a couple of mates and their son who is the same age as my boys. They had a 'mud kitchen' where you could make mud pies and generally muck about and get dirty with buckets and spades and rakes and leaves. I thought it looked fun and my mates' son agreed. Within about ten minutes, their boy was covered in mud from head to toe, having the time of his life. My two, however, just stood there and stared at the other children like they were aliens, and burst into tears every time a speck of mud hit their hands or face.

We ended up going home early – partly because my two were being such a complete nightmare and partly because we were expected to sit around a campfire and sing Nepalese folk songs as a group of women in stripy leggings attempted to make a soup out of a bag full of sweet potatoes, a couple of carrots and a very large cauliflower.

Forest school wasn't for me either.

It's odd how much my children like *being outside* but hated every natural thing that the outside world entailed. The other blinding contradiction was that the little one, who was as perturbed by dirt and leaves etc.

as his brother, had nevertheless absolutely no problem shoving every last thing he came across outdoors into his mouth.

I have never seen a child so orally fixated as him. If he wasn't eating (snacks of his choosing, naturally), which he liked to do every thirty minutes or so, he had something in his mouth. We were constantly fishing stuff out of there, you couldn't leave him for a minute without him licking, chewing or sucking on something he shouldn't.

On one occasion we were at a festival and we lost him briefly. We were slightly panicked until we saw him lying face down on a chalky pathway licking the stones. I don't know how long he had been there, but I do know people would have had to step over him to get past.

If I needed to get the boys out of the house, the usual solution, of course, was a trip to the local park or to one of Brighton's many public playgrounds. Playgrounds are tedious, but they have their upsides. Our boys liked them because the surface was reassuringly man-made, thus largely mud- and leaf-free. I liked then because they're free and you don't have to talk to anyone, mainly because you're too busy trying to stop your kid hurling themselves off the top of a slide.

I'm pretty sure I've been to every last playground in Brighton and Hove and they are all variables of the same thing: being Brighton, almost all of them have some kind of boat and beach theme. The reason I have been to so many is to provide something resembling variety to my everlasting day. I don't know why I bother because, essentially, it's the same old rigmarole in all of them.

Here's the routine. The boys ... try to climb the climbing frame (they can't because they can only just walk); try to walk across the bridge to the slide (impossible without holding my hand); try to run to the sand pit (but they have next to no balance, so I run behind them and watch them hit the deck every few feet). At some point, even if it hasn't rained for weeks, one of them will find a puddle, fall into it and need dry clothes. Throw several revolting nappy changes and the likelihood that I've forgotten their lunch / wet wipes / spare clothes / milk / water into the mix and, well, you can imagine the fun we're all having.

Then there are the outings to farms. Sussex is a hot-bed of farms – they're everywhere. I'll be honest with you: I'd never really been to a farm before my children were born. Now, I think I've been to about forty of them. Middle-class white people love nothing more than paying to take their children on tractor rides, out into the fields to stroke llamas and to watch the joy on their child's face when they see a pig for the first time ... blah blah blah.

The first time my two boys went to a farm, I'm not exaggerating when I say that they nearly shit themselves when they saw a horse. It's hardly surprising, given how small they were and how massive the horse was. It definitely traumatised them, because for quite a while afterwards, even saying the word 'horse' made them both start to convulse with fear.

Having spent most of my life living in London, farms were a bit of a novelty and I quite enjoyed our first few outings. By the eighth or ninth visit, however, the novelty had definitely diminished. How many goats does any one person need to see in a lifetime? And call me paranoid, but given how much the little one liked to lick walls, fences and milking parlour floors, I had to spend most of every visit trying to stop him from getting E. coli.

One winter weekend, we were staying in Bath with some friends whose son is about the same age as our boys, therefore an obligatory farm trip was on the cards. I had been working the night before so I felt exhausted (no change there), and an icy wind cut straight through our winter coats and hats as we trudged round that God-forsaken farmyard. As I stood in the dung with the wrong shoes on, wrapping my arms around my body to keep warm, I noticed a baby goat curled up in a little ball, sound asleep. Being tired and cold is not a great cocktail and when I saw that goat sleeping, I remember thinking, 'I wish I was that goat.'

You know your quality of life has dipped when you're looking at a goat asleep in what is essentially hay and its own excrement and you realise that a goat's quality of life is better than yours.

The pinnacle, the tippity-top, the winner of Worst Experience Ever for any parent, however, goes to soft play.

Soft play can fuck right off.

Soft-play centres are where you go when you have exhausted every other possible option of where to take your kids. No one in a soft-play centre is there because they want to be there. No one. Every single parent has a look of defeated resignation on their faces as they follow their child through a plastic tunnel, clamber up rubber stairs, over rope bridges and down slides that no adult should attempt without the appropriate padded onesie.

These places are always called things like, 'The Fun Factory' or 'Monkey Fun' or 'Fun Play'. Which is ironic really because I think I'd have more fun having the end of my nipples shaved off with a scythe than at any soft-play centre I've ever been to.

The first time we went we were lulled into a false sense of security because they were only a year old. At that age, there were only a few areas where they were allowed to go, so Chloe and I found ourselves sitting on a padded floor and having a relatively relaxing time, as we watched our boys scramble over padded bricks and shapes, or in and out of a small ball pit.

Fast-forward one year, and I found myself clawing my way along a padded corridor, trying to catch one of my boys as he hurtled through and over rubber shapes to the opening of a twisting plastic tunnel that would eventually spit him out into a ball pit at the bottom.

At the mouth of this tubular chute, I made eye contact with another mum.

'You're not going down there, are you?'

'Um yeah, he wants to go, so I have to go with him.'

She looked at me with a face that had seen too much. 'Don't go. I've been down that one and you don't want to go down there.'

Oblivious to my anxiety, my son was already ready to push himself down this cylindrical torture pipe, so readying myself, I grabbed him between my legs and down we went.

I don't know how long we spent during our descent. Like a solitary sports sock at the end of a spin cycle, my middle-aged self was slammed from one plastic side to the next, until I was eventually spat out the bottom like a sack of spuds, to the sound of my son shouting, 'AGAIN MAMA! AGAIN!'

I'd like to say that was the one and only time I made that mistake, but after that I went down another *four times*. I'm pretty sure part of my spleen is still up there.

Let's just hope they're over soft play before I hit my fifties and I permanently compact my spine.

Once my boys started to run it meant that I also had to run. I don't like running. I can run and I will run for a bus/train/plane or if I'm late for a meeting/casting/wedding, otherwise it's not for me.

By the time the bigger one was fifteen months old, he could run pretty quickly. Granted I'm faster than him – I should be, for heaven's sake, his legs are three times shorter than mine – but it's not just him I have to run after, there's also the little one to catch. As when they started crawling, they never run in the same direction. It's like they've planned it before we leave the house.

'Wait until she's turned her back, then you sprint towards the road and I'll run in the opposite direction towards the pond. She won't know which way to go! HA HA HA HA HA!'

Oh, how we laughed. Fast-forward a year and we bought them scooters for their second birthday (you have to, it's obligatory). I decided to take them to Rottingdean, a small seaside town nearby, so they can scoot along the seafront without having to worry about cars and too many pedestrians.

So, happy days, they were scooting about, but they still hadn't quite got the hang of steering, or stopping, or staying on the scooter, you know, the basics. Anyway, I was jogging along behind them when the little one fell off. He was fine, in fact, he was not hurt at all, but he'd had enough of the scooter so he abandoned it and sprinted off ahead. The bigger one was now also ahead of me so I started to run.

Given how small he is, the little one can really move. His scooter had meanwhile somehow also gained its own momentum and was heading towards a flight of steps down to the beach about ten feet below. I picked up my pace and ran towards the scooter to grab it before it fell, but as I did this, I saw my son running towards an identical set of steps further up the beach. I had to get to him before he fell and broke his head open, but the scooter was right there within reach.

Now, my thinking was that I should really grab the scooter because it was very expensive, also it was on the way to catching him. So, as I ran to grab it, I looked up to see an elderly couple standing in front of the little one, and blocking his fall to the beach below. I was out of breath, the scooter in my hand and I couldn't help but be aware of how this looked.

'Oh, thank you ... sorry bit out of breath ...'

[Painful silence.]

' ... with hindsight I probably should have grabbed him first ...'

The couple looked at me with two of the most withering stares I have ever received as an adult. I admit that from the outside looking in, that was not great PR as far as my parenting skills go, but I still maintain that I would have got to him in time and you, Reader, cannot dispute that, because you weren't there.

So there.

Also, before you start to judge any of my stupid actions in this chapter, just remember the level of exhaustion we're talking about here, will you? BECAUSE THEY STILL WEREN'T SLEEPING! I'll get back to that in a minute, trust me ...

They were still not great at eating either. Even though they'd both been successfully and fully weaned by now, they were both still highly opinionated, and highly vociferous selective eaters.

I shouldn't take it personally (I do), after all, most children are fussy eaters, but the little one is the fussiesr of the two and every meal time feels like a battle of wills as we try and find new and innovative ways to make him eat his dinner. At least the bigger one will eat something if you spoon it into his mouth, but the little one. THE LITTLE ONE IS DOING OUR RESPECTIVE HEADS IN.

Apparently, I'm not allowed to get annoyed or upset when my children refuse to eat, even though, as I've already explained, it's one of the few ways I can reassure myself that I'm doing something right. Making sure your kids eat is a bare minimum require-ment as far as parenting goes. And yet I'm convinced it would be easier to explain quadratic equations to a squirrel with ADHD than get my boys to finish their dinner.

I honestly wouldn't put up with this from anyone else. Imagine if you'd cooked a meal, maybe invited some friends over, and as you bring the dinner to the table one of your friends says, 'Euuuuurgh! No! I don't want it!'

Imagine then, that your friend then grabs a spoon and throws it at your head. Maybe you hand the spoon back to your friend and, say, not unreasonably, 'Don't throw your spoon, please.'

Your friend looks at you, directly in the eye, and throws the spoon again, this time hitting the wall behind you. You don't react, instead you pick up the spoon and say, 'Now, are you hungry?'

'Noooooooooo!' your friend screams.

'OK. So, why don't you just eat a bit of it?'

You watch your friend swipe the dinner you have lovingly prepared on to the floor. You both stare at the plate now resting upside down and your friend looks at you, smiles and shouts:

'BISCUIT!!!'

We all know where that biscuit would end up.

It's hard to reason with a toddler. They're just not up for it. Reason isn't something they've got to grips with. Most toddlers, in fact, haven't got to grips with any of the basics of the socialisation process. Remorse, boredom, anger control, impulse control and basic empathy? Forget about it! If you have a toddler in your house right now, you are basically living with a psychopath.

I look forward to the day I develop the 'the look'. My mum had it. She could just give us one look and we knew that if we didn't stop whatever we were doing there would be big trouble. She still has it, actually, now I come to think of it. I can give my boys 'the look' for hours and they just laugh in my face, usually as they're chewing on a laptop cable or trying to push my mobile phone through the floorboards. I have all the authority of a bewildered supply teacher in a borstal. No one's listening.

Fortunately, Chloe and I are always on the same page and incredibly supportive of one another.

'Are you giving him a biscuit?'

'It's just one biscuit.'

'I just told him he couldn't have a biscuit, so if you give him a biscuit, you're undermining my authority.'

'What authority?'

She's got a point.

I also found that it wasn't massively inspiring to try to get any good news or optimism on the subject of mealtime from mates with kids:

'Oh my God. It was a nightmare, Charlie only ate bananas until he was five.'

'My kids have never listened to a word I say, it's so depressing.'

'Kids are bastards, I wish I'd never had mine.'

Good times.

Reader, forget what I said earlier about people who offer unsolicited advice, unlike my not-so-upbeat mates, I'm going to offer you a helping hand, because that's the kind of supportive person I am. You're welcome.

So, if your baby / toddler / fifteen-year-old kid isn't eating your food, here are some helpful tips:

1. Don't take it personally (yeah right) – rejecting food is part of your child's development and goes towards learning about boundaries. (They also love to watch you squirm.)

2. If your child tries macaroni cheese and absolutely hoovers it down, don't be alarmed if they reject it the next time you dish it up and then refuse to even look at macaroni cheese for another six or seven years.

3. Don't panic if your child doesn't like his/her vegetables. It's perfectly normal. Keep offering them broccoli and after about fifty-eight attempts and them throwing it in your face, you'll start eating it thus contributing to *your* five a day.

4. If, after lovingly cooking another meal, you find that it has not been touched by your child, I can highly recommend comfort eating. Yes, you'll probably have your own dinner at the normal time of 8pm, but why not eat your kid's dinner too? It seems a shame to waste it.

5. If your child rejects your delicious first dinner menu, don't scramble around trying to make something else you think/hope they might like. They won't like it, but they will enjoy watching you make pasta and pesto in a state of heightened panic for the eleventh day in a row.

6. Make sure you have lots of cheese (cream cheese, Cheddar cheese, Babybel, Dairylea ...) along with hummus in the fridge at all times. Oh, and rice cakes. Or if you run out of rice cakes, just grab some polystyrene out of the recycling. They won't notice the difference.

7. No child will ever starve him-/herself. Children will eat when they're hungry. That's when you bring out the broccoli again. SUCKERS!

8. It turns out that when broccoli is the only option, certain children, who will remain nameless, are indeed happy to starve themselves.

9. Remember, always adhere to Tip Number 5.

10. OK, fine. It's pasta and pesto. AGAIN.

Did I mention that by their second birthday the boys were still not sleeping?? It was fine, though. FINE. Sleep's overrated anyway, I had decided. I actually grew to like the taste of Red Bull and spooning coffee granules straight into my mouth. Who cares that Chlo and I aged dramatically in that time? It was FINE. We were both FINE.

JUST FINE.

We were so lucky and we knew it. We had two happy boys who seemed to be enjoying life. They were miraculously unscathed, in fact, in spite of their zero-broccoli intake and lack of sleep. Whatever we were doing, they seemed positively thriving and healthy, really. That's not to say we hadn't had our fair share of accidents.

There was the time I slammed the bigger one's finger in a door. (Yeah, I did that.) At this point he could crawl and stand and was always getting under my feet. I remember seeing him standing by the kitchen door with his hands in the gap where the hinges are and picking him up and moving him away from the door. I also remember several minutes later, slamming that same kitchen door without looking to see where my son was, only to discover that he was where he had been just minutes before: at the door, with his fingers now stuck in the hinges. It was only after retrieving his fingers that I realised I'd nearly taken the middle one right off. The panic and immediate guilt I felt was intense, to put it mildly. I honestly thought I'd taken his finger right off because the top joint had all but disappeared. Fortunately for him and for me, his finger quickly reappeared, and I realised I'd just badly bruised it. So, not so bad really.

He won't remember.

Unless he reads this.

I mean, what are the chances?

There were other such horrendous incidents. There was the time when they were still small babies and I was lying on my back and I lifted the bigger one over my head like he was an aeroplane and he got overly excited. He wriggled out of my hands and just before he was about to land on his head, I caught him. But I caught him in an awkward way and I thought I'd dislocated his arm, resulting in a trip to A&E. Bad, eh? Well, it gets worse. That evening, I was booked to MC at a gig in Tunbridge Wells and rather than cancel the gig and explain to the promoter they would have to find someone else at very short notice, I left and went to my gig, leaving Chloe alone with our two baby boys, one of whom I had just injured and needed hospital attention.

Did I mention I took the car so Chloe had to get them on her own to A&E in a taxi?

Yeah, I did that.

Then there was the time that we took the boys swimming and I put the bigger one (yes, him again) on his back on a bench to get his nappy off, and turned briefly to grab a swim nappy only to find that he had rolled off the bench and landed chin-first on the tiled floor.

The first two accidents had been bad enough, but at least they had happened in the privacy of our house when I was on my own. At the swimming pool, I had an audience of about six other mums, who, even if they weren't judging me, were plainly indulging in some heavy-duty schadenfreude.

You know what they say, unfortunately for my son, these things happen in threes!

Like I said, apart from a nearly severed finger, a dislocated arm and a minor head injury, he's barely got a scratch on him.

Not that the little one escaped completely unscathed either: there was the time I tried to cut his fingernails and missed the nail completely and sliced into the top of his finger. It's FINE, it's all fine. These things happen.

Well, at least they do when I'm around.

The main thing is that they're happy and healthy, right? And given how often I have them on my own, I think that, stats-wise, I'm still doing OK.

I did feel terrible every single time. It's hard not to, they're tiny, vulnerable little bubs who wholly rely on you to keep them safe, so when you're the person who is responsible for their pain, it's a hard pill to swallow. You might say, harder for them – I think the jury's still out.

I'm not the mum I thought I would be. I get it wrong a lot of the time. I'm not perfect. I used to feel guilty about that most of the time, but now I think I'm reconciled with my shortcomings. None of us are the parents we thought we'd be, because it's not possible to be *that* bloody perfect.

I'm doing my best.

By the time the boys were nearly two, they were gabbling and forming words. The bigger one was speaking full sentences of utter gibberish while the little one preferred to pick a word and use it whenever he could – usually 'biscuit'. You spend months and months wondering what they'll say when they can finally speak to you and then they start talking and you'd wish they'd shut up.

'MUM, MAMA, MAMA, MUM, MAMA, MUM, MAMA, MAMA, MUM!'

'JESUS CHRIST! WHAT IS IT?'

'My biscuit is broken, can I have another one?'

'No, there's nothing wrong with it, just eat it.'

'IT'S BROKEN, MAMA! I DON'T WANT IT! I WANT ANOTHER ONE!'

'What are you upset about? It tastes the same and, look, you've got two biscuits now …'

'N O O O O O O O O O O O O O O! AAAAAAAAAAAAAARRRRRRGGGGGHHHH!'

[Watch as broken biscuit flies through the air and hits the wall.]

You gotta love them, otherwise you'd lock them in the cupboard and go to the pub.

By two and a bit, they were both talking volubly and were able to interact with us so much more, so it became a little easier to make them laugh or distract them when they were bored. But once they were talking, that could also be exhausting, and children don't have an off switch. There were many times when I simply wanted them to stop talking and just shut up.

That feeling doesn't go away – there are days when the most love I feel for them is when they are asleep. As they lie dormant, something about their angelic faces can make you forget that they've done nothing all day but kick, scream, fight, shout and talk to you like you're a trainee waiter in a TGI Fridays.

'I DON'T WANT ORANGE JUICE! I WANT APPLE JUICE!'

'Yes, Master! I'm so, so sorry that I didn't anticipate your EVERY WAKING NEED!'

Sometimes, as they chatter away incessantly, I find myself having to stop from downright ignoring them when they attempt to get my attention.

'Mama! Listen to me! Mama! I'm trying to tell you something really important!'

'Sorry, darling. I am listening. What is it?'

'Spiderman is having a birthday party and Iron Man and Superman are coming and so is Father Christmas.'

'That sounds wonderful …'

Some days, it's hard to feign interest in the social lives of various superheroes, but I do try to care and invest in the story. Although, I have noticed that by the time they get to about four years old, there is no point in trying to get too involved.

'Is Spiderman going to invite Batman?'

'No, Mama! Spiderman doesn't like Batman.'

'Oh, OK. Well, maybe they can play a game of musical statues?'

'They don't *like* musical statues, they like *pass the parcel*! Can you make Spiderman a pass the parcel?'

'I don't think so ...'

'But, Mama! It's his birthday!'

Please don't roll your eyes like that, I didn't make him a pass the parcel, I'm not that much of a pushover![1]

I know I'm a mug, of course I am. I'm in love with the little buggers, but I'm also so acutely aware of where I'm falling down as a parent that I'm sometimes inclined to overcompensate in other areas.

I'm not a 'creative' person; I know that sounds weird because I'm a stand-up comedian and I've clearly written this book![2] That side of creative stuff I can handle – but when it comes to anything artsy and crafty, I am *way* out of my depth. I just can't do it. When they were babies and I tried to do hand prints

---

[1] I am and it took ages.

[2] God, I really hope I have because it's hard to know if you'll ever finish it when you're actually writing it. If you're reading this then, 'Well done me!' If I'm reading this in a folder headed 'Things to finish before you die' then you, Jen Brister, are a bloody waste of space and I hope you're enjoying eating cold soup out of a tin somewhere off the M25, YOU IDIOT!

with them, I failed at that. At the end of the afternoon we had nothing to show for it: I couldn't even get a single clear thumb print from either of them. In the end, I just let them swirl their hands in paint and smear it wherever they wanted to. I have no capacity to come up with new and innovative ways to make stuff or draw stuff, or mould stuff with play dough. I am so bad at it, I've given up even trying. I have accepted I have no talent for it and have lived my life quite happily not being able to draw, or sew, or create anything practical with my hands. I am not a hands-on woman.

Chloe can't get her head round how bad I am at anything arty. There's nothing she likes more than 'making stuff'. She makes birthday cards and Christmas cards, advent calendars and birthday decorations. She gets a kick out of it and she's good at it! The woman has a degree in fine art! I got an E in my art GCSE. Yes, an E. I don't know anyone else who failed Art in my year. I only took it because I thought it would be easy. It wasn't easy, it was a bloody nightmare trying to screen-print the image of a forest that I couldn't draw in the first place. I was the only GCSE student in my year whose artwork wasn't displayed for the final presentation. My teacher actually asked me not to put it up because she didn't want to be associated with the crap I'd produced. I was relieved. I didn't want to be associated with it either.

I'm much better at 'being a monster' or 'a horse', or anything that involves being a climbing frame. In fact, I'll happily climb a tree with them or hunt for the Gruffalo, or build a den, anything really, just as long as I never ever have to make a Christmas decoration out of an ice lolly stick, a pine cone and some glitter.

17

You've Got This

By the time the children were walking and talking, I was ready to see the back of nappies. Having nailed the weaning lark, more or less, potty-training was, as far as I was concerned, the last big hurdle. Having spent two whole years up to my neck in poo, I couldn't wait to see the back of nappies.

For me, nappies symbolised the nadir of life with twins. For one thing, they're not cheap, and when you have two babies, you go through a lot of them: I mean *a shitload*. I hate to think of our contribution to the mountain of non-biodegradable nappies that are currently lying *not* rotting in a landfill somewhere. Yes, we are those people – the ones that fastidiously recycle their plastic, but then dump all their shitty nappies in the ground and pray that it doesn't have a horrific and irreversible effect on the environment.[1]

At the beginning, we had had the best of intentions. We tried cloth nappies (for about a week) but we just couldn't get to grips with them. Our two shat themselves every three hours at the least, and the cloth nappies never seemed to contain the wee, never mind the poo. They leaked everywhere, so we not only had to change the nappies, but also their baby grows and their blankets. We went through them at such a rate that we would have needed to buy at least forty of the bastards, because you can't just stick them in the washing machine when they're caked in excrement – you have to soak them in a bucket with bicarbonate of soda, then rinse them, *then* wash them, and then wait for about a week until they were properly dry and frankly we didn't have the money, time, inclination or energy for it. There are plenty of women who do and I'm sure there are also mums of twins who manage to cope with washing and drying every single dirty nappy, but Chloe and I quickly realised that we are not those mums; we are pragmatic, no-nonsense women who love a shortcut. You know: NORMAL MUMS.

I'm not a fan of poo. I'm not even that enamoured with my own poo, if I'm honest. I like to do

[1] It does.

one a day (maybe two if I'm hungover), and flush it down the loo. I don't want to examine it, or get in among it, check its consistency, or odour. I'm in, then I'm out.

A year into motherhood and I was very much at home among the poo and the wee. I was a nappy-changing machine. By that age, I had effectively dealt with what felt like hundreds of thousands of nappies.

I wasn't even that bothered by it, not at first. As newborns, their full nappies were so benign: if your baby is breastfed, early on their poo kind of smells like digestive biscuits. It was relatively inoffensive really. They just pooed and wee-ed in this mild-mannered way all day and all night long. A lot of the time, as far as I could see, that was their main pastime.

So far, I'd only been exposed to the mild odour of milky poo. I'm not saying that I liked it or that I looked forward to changing their nappies because it smelled great – it really didn't. But it was not like an adult poo. Adult poos are … Well, I don't need to tell you what they're like, you have one every day, you know what I'm talking about!

The day we started weaning the boys was a poo game-changer. The instant you start feeding your child solids is the instant that *their* solids go up to the next level – and by that, I mean, their shit STINKS. Let me tell you, it's a sad day when you go to change your baby son's nappy and you're confronted with what looks and smells like something your dad once did on Boxing Day after one too many slices of turkey washed down by one too many glasses of port. It is, to all intents and purposes, a bloody horror show.

The first time I opened a nappy and was confronted by such a monstrosity, I couldn't reconcile my beautiful baby boy with the horror he had just evacuated. Surely my eyes shouldn't be watering like this? Do I still have eyebrows? On the plus side, my sinuses cleared up.

You put up with stuff that, prior to having kids, you would never have entertained for more than a second; the compromises you make when you have children are quite frankly insane. Take, for example, the time that Chlo asked me to sniff her jeans.

'Why?'

'I think they've got piss on them. I just want to know how bad it smells.'

I want you to know that, prior to having children, neither Chloe nor I would *ever* have contemplated leaving the house with urine on our jeans. Fast-forward ten months and neither of us had the energy to give a toss. All I can tell you is that, worn down, sooner or later by a certain stage your standards slip, then finally drop to a depth that you couldn't have fathomed just a year earlier.

Here's something that I seemed to get to grips with very quickly: having poo under my nails. (NB: See Chapter 11 for a more graphic description.) Now, I know some of you are going to read this and visibly wince, as you should. There is nothing OK about having poo under your fingernails. Before having the boys, had I found a speck of faeces on my hands, I would have been scrubbing them in the sink with a wire brush and some bleach. Now when I find poo under my nails, I find myself saying, 'What is that? Is that ... poo?' Then I scrape it out with my thumbnail and carry on with my day.

Several months into weaning and aged forty-one, I found myself in my house having a tantrum – an actual full-blown tantrum. Yeah, yeah. Judge away, but let's not forget we have twins, so we have double the amount of EVERYTHING. Which means that on a daily basis we have a lot of poo coming out of our house. And I mean A LOT. I don't know if I've emphasised this enough, but if not, listen up.

On this particular day when I had the tantrum, I found myself in my living room shouting at Chloe who was upstairs.

'Why does the living room smell of poo?'

'WHAT?'

'WHY DOES OUR LIVING ROOM STINK OF POO? HAVE THE WALLS OF THIS HOUSE FINALLY JUST ABSORBED THE SMELL?'

Chloe, as always, was busy with more important things and, frankly, was not taking me seriously. So I wandered into the kitchen muttering to myself.

'Hang on, why does the kitchen stink of poo? Have our hygiene levels dropped so dramatically that we're OK with our kitchen smelling of actual crap? I mean, what if someone comes over? Are we going to offer them a cup of tea and a shit sandwich?!'

I stormed up the stairs.

'Chloe, the stairwell stinks! What the hell is wrong with this house?'

By this point I was apoplectic and as I reached our bedroom I finally lost it.

'WHY DOES OUR BEDROOM SMELL OF POO? HOW IS IT THAT THE ONE PLACE WHERE WE NEVER HAVE A SINGLE NAPPY STINKS OF SHIT?! I CANNOT LIVE LIKE THIS A SECOND LONGER!'

Moments later, when I went into the bathroom and looked in the mirror, I realised I had poo on my chin.

I said to Chloe, 'How long have I had shit on my face?'

'Ages.'

'When were you going to tell me?'

'I dunno. I just assumed you knew it was there.'

I didn't realise that things had gotten so bad that Chlo thought I was fine about having poo on my face.

It's pretty hard to claw back any dignity from that point.

Fortunately, although in denial, Chloe's standards had dropped as far as mine, as I pointed out to her after I'd let her walk through the streets of Brighton with sick all down her back.

Yes, I do hold a grudge.

The endless nappies were such a pain in the arse that we couldn't wait to eventually start potty training. We naively thought the grass would be greener. It wasn't. Just you try introducing the concept of 'no more nappies' to someone who has spent their days pooing at will, whenever and wherever they like. It doesn't work.

In the end, we didn't bother to try to potty-train them until they were two and a half and even then we were only nappy-free when we were at home. It was the summer so they were naked most of the time anyway and we could introduce their potty as and when they looked like they needed it. Most of the time it was a guessing game, but one that we got pretty good at. One afternoon, Chloe was sitting with them on the sofa reading them a story, when the little one stood up. With a mother's instinct, Chloe stuck out her hand and caught his poo before it hit the ground. That's what being a mum is: catching a turd in your hand and not batting an eyelid. She was so proud!

'Jen, I literally caught it IN MY HAND!'

'That's great, love.'

'Honestly, it was massive!'

'Can we possibly finish this conversation after dinner?'

'You don't think it's going to be that warm ...'

When we were potty-training, it was not unusual to find a poo in your shoe, behind the sofa, or by the radiator, or in the middle of the bathroom floor; we were just grateful if it was a wipeable surface.

The difficulty with potty-training, though, wasn't that. It was fine when we were at home: they could have as many accidents as they wanted at home, because we were armed with disinfectant, rubber gloves and a stack of antibacterial wipes. The problem was when we left the house.

That's the key to potty-training: NEVER EVER LEAVE YOUR HOME.

To be honest, it doesn't really matter how long you wait to risk it without a nappy outside of the house, you're never going to get the timing right. Your child might have used her potty successfully all week, she knows what she's doing, she is confident and happy and very excited about wearing her new favourite knickers. As a parent, you're thrilled. It's all gone so smoothly. You have nailed potty-training. WELL DONE, YOU!

Except that you haven't nailed it at all, because ten minutes after reaching your destination, you start to notice a bit of a whiff and there's a great big poo falling out of those favourite pants. Look, don't worry about it. We've all been there. I've been there A LOT and a few times I've been there without the necessary equipment.

I was so happy that we finally had no more nappies to take everywhere, but there is still a lot of crap you have to take with you until they're old enough to use the toilet. Even at two years of age, they are not ready for that. What you have to do is take your own toddler-size toilet with you – a portable potty with disposable poo bags as well as wet wipes and at least four different changes of clothing. I'll be honest with you, this did not feel like progress.

The number of times I managed to leave the house without the portable potty are too embarrassing to recall. I do, however, have a lasting memory of being at my local park with my kids and on this occasion, you'll be pleased to hear that I had remembered the potty. I took my son behind a tree and he proudly did his business and I proudly looked on, knowing that this time I was a hero because I had come prepared. No medals necessary, I'm just an ordinary working mum being pretty brilliant on a day-to-day basis.

'FINISHED, MAMA!' shouted my son.

I went to wipe his bum. I looked in my bag and I didn't have any wet wipes. I scrabbled about a bit in the bag. I didn't have any tissue paper, or any kind of absorbent material at all. I also didn't have a change of clothing so I couldn't use his pants to wipe his bum. So, I rummaged through the bag again, picking up random things and wondering if I could use any of them to wipe my son's bum.

'OK, I've got a plastic bottle ... no, that's not going to work. A very small receipt? Nope, that'll just slide off. How about this credit card?'

Honestly, there was nothing there. I did contemplate my sleeve for longer than I like to admit, but even I had to conclude that was a terrible idea. I could see a group of mums in the distance with children about the same age as mine and I thought, 'I could just go over and ask them for a wet wipe. I mean, we've all been there, right? They'll totally understand ... God, they look so happy, why are they laughing so much? Who laughs when they've got children? Hang on ... Is she wearing LIP GLOSS?'

Fuck it. Plan B.

I did what any decent parent with low self-esteem would do in my situation: I lifted my son up under his legs and dragged his tiny bum along the grass. Kerching! Clean as a whistle.

And if some of you are thinking, how humiliating,[2] get over it: the great thing about being two years old is that there is very little if anything that can embarrass you, including having your poo-covered bum trailed through foliage.

Anyway, it could be worse, he could have pooed himself in soft play! Ha ha ha. Imagine that?[3]

---

[2] You, thought I was referring to myself, didn't you? Well, you'd be wrong, 'cos you can't humiliate someone who has chosen that as a means of making an honest living.

[3] Yes one of them shat himself in soft play. Look, these places ARE NOT HYGIENIC and don't think for a second my son is the first kid to do it. That ball pit is in fact a BACTERIA pit.

241

18

Happy Holidays

If you are in any doubt, any doubt at all, as to just how much your life has changed after becoming a parent, then can I suggest you go on a family holiday? The reality that your holiday is not actually a holiday, but in fact an endurance test in a different place without all your usual home comforts, becomes apparent all too quickly.

I think that even up until the boys were about three, we were still a little bit in limbo, but in the first year, we were definitely just sort of reeling about. Neither of us had quite got our heads round the fact that we wouldn't be able to live our lives as we had before. We were still learning the hard way that life was not what it had been, which might explain why we thought it would be a brilliant idea to venture on our first ever family holiday when the boys were only eight months old. Nothing helps to focus your mind more than a week away with two small babies.

We didn't go abroad in the first year, we didn't really have the money and in fairness I would rather have had my face dragged down a pebble-dash wall than try and take two babies on a plane anywhere. Instead, to recapture a bit of coupley romance, we had hired a cottage for a week in Dorset. I don't know what I thought it was going to be like, maybe I still deludedly thought it would be a holiday. Ha ha ha!

No.

I was so excited when I booked that cottage – it looked so quaint and romantic online, with lots of small nooks and little rooms to relax in on a comfy sofa, and read a book with a glass of wine. All of this would have been great had it been just the two of us, or even if we'd gone with friends, but our companions were two eight-month-old babies and, if anything, the holiday just seemed to unsettle them.

The other thing you have to factor in when you go anywhere with a baby is the amount of stuff you have to take with you. Buggy, baby slings, clothes, nappies, wipes, nappy cream, high chairs, travel cots, food, toys, a bath mat, bottles, formula, steriliser, plastic bowls, spoons ... now multiply that by two!

243

It's a military operation trying to leave the house for an hour, let alone for a week. I am so thankful that I am with a woman who knows how to write a list, transfer that list on to an excel spreadsheet, cross-reference that spreadsheet and basically pack everything. I find loading the car stressful enough.

That week felt LONG and not in a good way. Cho and I weren't able to indulge in our usual holiday treats like long lunches, walks in the countryside, evenings out in a local pub or restaurant. As it turns out, babies don't enjoy doing ANY OF THOSE THINGS. In fact, they would much prefer it if you didn't go on holiday at all because they actually like what they know, which is home.

I'm sure we had fun at some point, I'm sure we did. Looking back at the photos of that week, you could be fooled into thinking we had the time of our lives! But the truth is, it was hard. The boys were still WIDE awake every morning between 4 or 5am. We were taking it in turns to let the other one lie in, but the mornings I had to get up with them felt interminable.

A big part of being a parent is killing time. I know that sounds terrible but it's the truth. Every day you wake up at 4/5/6am and you know that from that moment on, you're going to have to fill the day with stuff to do. When your children can't really speak yet, are not old enough to entertain themselves or each other for any length of time, but are both mobile, and you are but a shell of the person you used to be, those early mornings are probably the closest thing to hell on earth we mums will know.

CBeebies is your friend.

I really don't care what anyone says about how much screen time babies should have. I know you're not SUPPOSED to let your baby watch TV until they're two years old for developmental and blah blah blah reasons I've never bothered to properly look into. But the second those two boys could focus their eyes, we switched on the telly.

So, usually at 6am on the dot the telly is switched on; and briefly, maybe for fifteen minutes, maybe half an hour if we're lucky, our two boys will become mesmerised with the colourful images, songs and shapes on this magical box. Meanwhile, I will be able to lie very still on the sofa, trying not to think about how cosy, warm and sound asleep Chloe is in bed at this very moment.

We will watch all kinds of crap even after they have lost interest, I will keep it on in the background just for the company. Watching children's television when you are only semi conscious, in what feels like the middle of the night because it's still dark outside, is surreal. Everything feels unreal but heightened at the same time because children's television is bonkers on the whole and most of the presenters look like they're off their heads on something. I seriously tip my hat to any children's presenter because I could not maintain that level of wide-eyed enthusiasm for that long.

'Come on kids! Let's sing a song about autumn! What's your favourite leaf? Have *you* tried kicking leaves in your local park?'

MY KIDS DON'T LIKE LEAVES, OK? SO, NO; WE'RE CRAWLING THROUGH THE PARK AVOIDING LEAVES AND GRASS AND MUD AND ANY OTHER NATURAL SURFACES BECAUSE WE PREFER ASPHALT, CONCRETE AND RUBBER!

I think there should be a limit as to how long anyone can work in kids' TV before you're asked to leave. You can tell the people who have been doing it for too long because there is a discernible deadness behind the eyes that you just can't shake.

What I'm trying to say is that Mr Tumble is unsettling not just because he's a grown man pretending to be a child dressed as a clown, but also because I can't help thinking that for all the awards and accolades and piles of cash he has, the guy clearly hates his job.

Some of the shows that are for children border on nightmarish. Whoever came up with *Baby Jake* needs to have a long hard look at themselves and the Teletubbies clearly have something extra added to their custard.

I digress.

On holiday in Dorset, we didn't have all the toys and distractions we usually have. The cottage was far from baby-proofed and the TV didn't work so I couldn't even console myself with breakfast telly. The 4am–9am stint feels like FOREVER when you have no adult conversation, you're dead on your feet and you haven't got the energy to sing 'Incy Wincy Spider' or play peek-a-boo. Every morning I would find myself lying on a rug staring at my sons through heavy lids, praying that Chloe would miraculously wake up and save me from this fresh hell.

We went on day trips and there were a couple of visits to Corfe Castle and Lulworth that were fun, mainly because for once the kids weren't screaming 90 per cent of the day. But I also remember a really arduous trip to Lyme Regis that I could have done without. I think in our heads we thought a trip to a sandy beach would be fun for them, they could play in the sand, we could bring a picnic and sit on the beach and relax. I was also looking forward to being on a beach where I didn't have to constantly fish stones out of their mouths.[1]

I had it in my head that children LIKED beaches and they do, but babies, or at least our babies thought this beach outing in Dorset was some kind of horrific endurance test that we had subjected them and ourselves to for absolutely no reason. As I

---

[1] As on Brighton Beach, which is made entirely of delicious, yummy pebbles.

mentioned, we had noticed our sons' bizarre allergic reaction to any surface that wasn't man-made, and their utter abhorrence of grass, foliage and other trappings of the natural world. Yet, when we planned our beach outing, we hadn't even considered that they might have a problem with sand. Needless to say, they did. They had quite a big problem with it. They hated it, which with hindsight isn't a surprise, given that it sticks to your hands and feet, gets absolutely everywhere, is disgusting when it gets in your mouth and is a nightmare if it gets anywhere near your eyes. It didn't help that it was simultaneously blowing a gale so sand was flying directly into the boys' faces and I spent most of the time shouting expletives at seagulls who were trying desperately to nick our lunch.

About nine months later we tried again. This time we thought we were ready to try going on our first family holiday *abroad*.

As two mums, gay parents, in other words when you're considered part of a minority, you have to take so much more stuff into consideration. Even holidays abroad have to be chosen carefully.

'Have you thought about Dubai?'

'Dubai? No, aside from their questionable human rights record, the fact that the entire country is built on bonded labour, their attitude towards women and "foreigners" is appalling and being gay in Dubai is illegal, I haven't really thought about it as a holiday destination, mate.'

Here are some other countries I won't be visiting with my family: Afghanistan, Brunei, Saudi Arabia or Iran. I always find the death penalty for 'existing' a massive turn-off when it comes to picking a holiday.

I know it might sound like I'm being hyperbolic but I'm just taking the opportunity at this juncture to remind you, dear Reader, that when you're gay you're not having the same life experience as a straight person, that's all. I know it seems obvious but when you're not aware of your own privilege, sometimes it's helpful for a beige lesbian to remind you.

Our first holiday abroad *en famille*, therefore, was a jaunt to gay-friendly Portugal when the boys were eighteen months old. We managed to choose the only week in May in the last thirty years in Portugal when it was at least ten degrees colder than average, with virtually no sunshine.

'If you had been here last week it was twenty-four degrees! It's going to be thirty degrees next week!'

Yes, that's great to hear, thank you. Sadly, this week it's sixteen degrees, which is the exact same, positively chilly temperature as it is in Brighton.

The beaches nearby were sandy and we had brought buckets and spades with us in anticipation of us all making sand castles together as a family. Surely by now the boys would have got over their compulsive aversion to lovely white sand?

Nope.

The bigger one would not get off the towel, if his feet so much as grazed against the sand he was inconsolable. The little one could just about cope with being near sand if it meant he could put it in his mouth. You would think that after the first couple of times of putting sand in your mouth you'd think to yourself:

'That is disgusting, I'm not going to do that again.'

And, yes, he would think it was disgusting and he'd cry and get upset and we'd wipe the sand from his face, give him water to drink to get it all out of his mouth and give him a kiss to make him feel better.

Two seconds later, we'd turn round and see him shoving a handful of sand back into his mouth.

Even now the boys are older, despite all evidence to the contrary, we steadfastly cling on to that delusion that we can enjoy a family holiday. The truth is we haven't had an actual 'holiday' since the boys were born, because for me a holiday is a break away from work. What we have come to realise is that holidays aren't really holidays mainly because you've got to take your children with you and they ruin it.

These days, for me a holiday involves sleeping and not moving. I love not moving, preferably for as long as possible. I have to do a lot of moving with work. Driving miles to gigs or spending hours on trains, in airports, on boats.[2] So, when I'm not working, I like to do very little actual moving of any kind, which is completely impossible when you have children.

Last year when the boys were three, I finally had some money after my *Live at the Apollo* appearance so I decided I'd treat us to a week in an all-inclusive resort in Turkey. Reading about it and looking at the photos I thought, 'This looks great!' Even Chloe agreed that the resort looked perfect! So, I splashed a load of cash and off we flew.

I don't know if you've been to one of these places, but for the first twenty-four hours you think you're in paradise: everything is amazing and it feels like it's free.[3] That's until you realise the food is grim, the booze tastes weird and every night you're trapped in a hotel room with your children. By day three, it started to feel less like a holiday and more like I was in prison. To be fair Chlo enjoyed it, probably because we didn't have to DO anything.

It turns out not doing anything for a week isn't my bag after all.

I'm being slightly disingenuous when I say it was awful. There were loads of things to like; the weather, for one, because it was actually hot. There were plenty

---

[2] Maybe not boats.
[3] It's not free. Remember the shitload of cash you spent before you got there.

of pools for the kids to muck about in. At the age of three they had finally gotten over their sand phobia[4] so we could *almost* enjoy going to the beach. I say almost because the major downside of any kind of hot weather is sun cream.

Now, we all know how important it is to wear sun protection.[5] Try explaining that to a three-year-old. You'll find that their give-a-fuckometer doesn't flicker one bit. Putting sun cream on our children is even less fun than cleaning their teeth, which has on occasion required something close to a headlock[6] to achieve. As soon as our boys see the sun cream bottle, they leg it. I'm the one who has to run after them, of course. Now, I think we can also all agree that running in swimwear is a massive no-no, even if you're built like Pamela Anderson.[7] Indeed, it's hard to maintain any dignity or air of parental control, or authority when you're running after a three-year-old in very little clothing, as your thighs wobble and rub together and your boobs feel like they're going to bounce out of what little material is just about holding them in.

[4] There is a light at the end of the tunnel!
[5] Not all of us, clearly, we've all seen people on holiday sunbathing like it's a full-time job, proudly modelling a tan that makes them look like a walking, talking leather boot.
[6] No need to contact social services.
[7] OK, FINE, she did look great.

Once you eventually have got a hold of them you then have to brush enough sand off their skin so that you can attempt to slather factor fifty all over their body, ears and face. You might get as far as one leg, maybe even an arm before they sprint off again and you, fishing your swimsuit out of your arse and tucking a boob in, run after them. Repeat this nightmare scenario until their entire body is covered from head to toe in a layer of caked sand. I mean sun cream.

Happy holidays.

19

Babies: They Were Born This Way

My interest in fashion is pretty low. I do try to look good, *I do*, but my idea of looking good is sporting a clean shirt and jeans.

As a twenty-something I had no idea what I was doing: I look back at photos of myself and cringe. I remember buying a V-neck jumper and thinking it looked pretty good until I asked a mate's opinion. Her judgement was pretty conclusive:

'It's fine, Jen, if you want to look like Ronnie Corbett.'

Needless to say, I never wore it again. Needless also to say, no one has ever looked to me for fashion advice.

I own three pairs of jeans, a couple of pairs of trousers, a dozen shirts and some jumpers. That's it, that's me. The idea that our children become fashion accessories, therefore, really gets my goat. If I looked good, I wouldn't mind so much, because it would make sense to have children that dressed in a way that mirrored my own aesthetic. But the truth is, I don't look good. I spent the first two years of my boys' lives looking like a woman on the brink of a breakdown. I am now frequently to be seen staggering around the streets of Brighton in jeans that were clean at 7am that morning, but are now covered in a veritable Dulux colour-chart of stains.

Meanwhile, as a woman who can barely dress herself, I'm now somehow expected to choose 'outfits' for my children. That's right: 'outfits'. My sons now have more clothes than I do. Take a sneaky look in their bedroom, and their so-called 'wardrobe' would put most adults to shame. We were very lucky because most of their clothes were hand-me-downs from friends, and I am forever grateful to them. But then add a handful of clothes bought by friends and grandparents and our boys have more get-ups than Beyoncé.

Chloe takes the dressing of our children very seriously: colours need to coordinate; tops should, wherever possible, match socks; denim should be skinny or distressed; jumpers must be chunky and moustaches waxed.[1] Our boys should look like they're ready for a GAP photoshoot at any given moment. It's not just Chloe who does this; Brighton mums in general seem to be obsessed with dressing their toddler like they're a twenty-six-year-old hipster working in a vegan cafe.

I get that you want your kids to look good or at least clean (when you leave the house), but there have been days where my care factor about what the boys are wearing has barely registered. On days when I have actually tried to make an effort, where Chloe is concerned, I've still got it wrong.

'Why did you put him in that jumper?'

'He was wearing it yesterday.'

'Yes, but not with those trousers.'

'OK, I'll change his trousers. How about these?'

'No.'

'These ones?'

'No.'

'I quite like …'

'No.'

'YOU CHOOSE THEN!'

It's a bloody minefield.

---

[1] Yes, I am being facetious but I wouldn't put it past her.

Added to this, as a pair of left-leaning liberal lez-zas,[2] we are trying to ignore the societal pressures of bringing up our boys within the traditional gender norms. We really are pushing the colour pink and are prepared to buy princess dresses and glittery tops should our sons want to wear them. I know that Chloe is secretly hoping one of them will love girls' clothes, opening up an entirely new range of fashion for her to explore.

I have no problem with boys wearing girls' clothes or vice versa. I spent my childhood in boys' clothes and would wear more men's clothes if they fit me. Nonetheless, I confess that when it comes to buying any items of clothing for my children, I seem to find myself exclusively looking in the boys' section. Chlo, on the other hand, doesn't care whether it's in the boys' or girls' section, as long as the clothes look good.

Some people are really hung up on clearly sign-posting the gender of their children. You'll see it just walking down the street, babies being pushed in bright pink or blue prams. Maybe I'm the one making the assumption that they've chosen the colour based on the gender of their baby, though. Who knows?

---

[2] Chlo is actually bisexual but that just didn't fit in with my hilarious comedy alliteration.

It's Brighton, for heaven's sake, they may well be subverting gender norms and have bought a pink pram for their son.[3]

We didn't have a blue or a pink pram when the kids were babies, but Chloe did deliberately buy bright-pink sleeping bags for the buggy. Nine times out of ten people assumed that the contents of those two pink bags was two infant girls. When we corrected them, most people didn't bat an eyelid and just carried on cooing over them. On one occasion, though, as I was on one of my many early morning beachfront walks to get the boys to sleep, this bloke could not get his head round it:

'You put your boys in pink sleeping bags?'

'Yes.'

'Are you trying to give them a complex?'

'They're three weeks old. I don't think they have any concept of who they are, let alone what sex they are.'

'I'm telling you now, love, carry on like this and your boys are going to have problems.'

I felt like saying, 'Look, mate, carry on talking to me like that and you're going to get an angry, sleep-deprived lesbian shouting abuse directly into your stupid, ignorant face!'

---

[3] They haven't.

Instead, I didn't say anything, I was too tired. I just rolled my eyes and gave him the finger when he walked off.

Pre kids I remember buying three T-shirts for my friend's daughter. I didn't realise at the time, but they were boys' T-shirts.

'You're going to have to take these T-shirts back, Jen,' my friend said.

'Oh, don't you like them?'

'If you read the tag, they're actually boys' T-shirts.'

'She's one year old. I'm pretty sure she can't read yet.'

'I just don't want my daughter wearing boys' clothes, OK?'

I could understand if I'd turned up with a T-shirt that read, 'Daddy's Little Boy', but otherwise it seemed a bit of an overreaction.

When you use the logical side of your brain, there is absolutely no reason why people can't wear whatever the hell they like. As a society we have gendered absolutely *everything*: clothing, emotions and attitudes. Anyone who steps outside of these strict 'norms' is exposed to vilification and mockery at best, open discrimination at worst.

Right now, Chlo and I don't know what our kids' sexuality is, or how they might identify in terms of their gender as they get older; if they decide they were born a boy but have always felt like a girl, or have never identified as either gender, or if they're 100 per cent certain of who they are.

In terms of their sexuality, they might be gay, bi or completely asexual. Whoever they are, Chlo and I just want them to know that they will always be loved and accepted.

If you don't have children, you might think that as a parent you will be the one to shape your child's personality. You might think that their temperament, likes and dislikes are malleable and easy to mould.

Well, you'd be wrong.

Let me tell you, your baby comes out fully formed. I don't mean cognitively; I mean fully formed in terms of who they are and will become as people. Sure, you can influence your children, guide them, instil your values – but their 'personality' is there from the beginning.

For example, there is no way either of us is ever going to convince the bigger one to wear a dress, wear pink, or play with dolls. He's not interested. He likes trucks, diggers, cranes, lorries. Even when he was just a baby, he would squeal his head off in joy if he saw a building site or some full-on roadworks. He could watch a digger in the road for twenty minutes at a time and was devastated when we eventually turned the buggy to leave.

In many ways, he has all the attributes you would traditionally associate with being a boy. He could catch before he was two, he has great coordination, balance and spatial awareness. He loves puzzles and building things. He is great at climbing, jumping and running and had no problem learning to ride his scooter or bike. He is absolutely gorgeous and we know that he's going to be a bloody heartbreaker when he hits adolescence. Despite his seeming jock-like exterior he is also a sensitive soul and is always up for a cuddle.

Like his brother, the little one has great balance and spatial awareness and is a *really* fast runner, but he can't catch and has zero concentration or anything resembling an attention span. His favourite colours change daily but pink is often his colour of choice. He has a vivid imagination and loves nothing more than dressing up as a fairy, a ladybird or a magic bumblebee. He has no problem wearing a sparkly tutu and one of his favourite games is to play 'families' where he is always the 'baby sister'.

They have been these little individuals from birth: we have done very little to shape their personalities. We find it hard enough to get them to eat broccoli, so I don't know how we thought we'd be able to make them into the people we want them to be.

Once you accept that about your kids, there is a freedom that comes with it; as much as you discipline them, you can't fundamentally change who they are. If your kid is gay, trans, non-binary, easy-going, impatient, fun, serious, generous or stingy, they are that person from the GET-GO.

I find it so strange when some parents lose their shit when their kid comes out as trans, gay, bi, non-binary. Firstly, it's not a choice and, secondly, it's not ABOUT YOU. Maybe it's because I'm a non-biological parent, but biological parents need to be reminded that they've created a NEW PERSON. They're not a version of you, they are someone brand-new; while you may share genetics, that does not mean that you necessarily have anything else in common.

How many of us have spent time with our families and thought, 'How the hell am I related to any of you?' I say this as a gay woman. My gayness has nothing to do with my parents, not a thing. I know I was born this way, from a very young age I liked girls. I have never liked boys and believe me I tried. My parents could not have done anything to change that: it's just who I am, and that applies to almost every aspect of my personality. Of course, my mum tried to share her values and fuel my confidence so I could better achieve my goals. She loves all four of her children and she understood that we needed a good education, self-belief and opportunities. She always did her best to provide these, but she was never going to create who we are as individuals.

It's a big responsibility, being a parent. It can feel overwhelming if you think on it for any amount of time and it's often overshadowed by the practical side of just surviving the week. I know we're not perfect parents, I'm sure you've gleaned that much for yourself, but Chloe and I are doing our best. While we can't control who our children are, we want to make sure that we bring them up to be happy, that we can give them some kind of moral compass, teach them about empathy, kindness and compassion. We want our two boys to grow up to be two men who might actually like women; I feel like producing two feminists is the *very least* that Chlo and I can do as parents.

I don't want them to feel threatened by equality, to have skin so thin that they feel frightened and angry about anyone who doesn't look or behave exactly like they do.

We want our boys to feel like they can wear whatever clothes they want, identify as they choose and fall in love with whoever they want. Even if they feel like they can't always express who they are in the outside world, we want them to feel comfortable to be themselves when they're at home with us.

Sometimes it's hard to not give your children mixed messages. I want my boys to know that it's not OK for strangers to touch them or kiss them, or hold them if they don't want it, and yet the number of times I've found myself telling my kids to kiss a total stranger.

'Come on! Give Mike a kiss, go on! I know you don't want to and it feels weird and you'd rather play with your Lego but do it because Mama said so. Not on the cheek darling, on the lips!'

We've all been guilty of that, even if it's only once. Why do we do that? Tell our kids to be affectionate when they don't want to? Affection is spontaneous and organic, affection shouldn't need to be instructed. We have this societal expectation around being polite. Which is fine but when did kissing become an expression of politeness?

Which is why I think we should adopt the high five. It's mutual, it's quick, you're in, you're out. Really hard to make a high five creepy. I'm not saying it can't be done, I'm sure there'll be someone out there who'll give it a whirl.

'Mate, why is your hand coming towards my tits?'

I want them to feel confident with who they are so that they understand the importance of consent, not just for their partner but for themselves. I want to teach our boys that they have agency when it comes to their own bodies but also that they have to respect the agency of others.

I know it's not going to be easy, what with the internet and how simple it is for kids to access pornography. When I was growing up if you wanted to see a boob or a groin you had to make do with the Littlewoods catalogue. These days kids only have to get on to Google and they can watch any number of cocks being waved about or stuffed into any number of holes, some of which are clearly marked 'exit only'.

I'm not a prude, I know kids need to explore their sexuality, and for many boys porn, in particular, can be the first port of call. I know our boys are only four right now, but I genuinely worry about how I'm going to talk to them about sex. No one wants to talk to their parents about that sort of stuff.

'Now, Mum and I want to talk to you about sex.'

'No thanks.'

'OK, glad we had that talk.'

I'm not a fan of porn, again it's not that I'm a prude, I think sex is great and people going at it hell for leather and being paid, in principle, sounds like a great idea. But I've seen enough pornography to know it's not for me. I also know that it's not the place where I want my sons to learn about what women do and don't like.

Again, who wants to have THAT conversation with their son?

'Now, you've probably watched a fair bit of porn ...'

'NO, I HAVEN'T!'

'Look, I know you have because you never bother to wipe your search history.'

'MUM!'

'My point is, I've noticed that you've been looking at "Horny girls who take it any which way", and I just want you to know that women, generally speaking, don't like it any which way. At least, not until they're in a loving relationship and, even then, it's probably only for a short time, because it's knackering and you're not as flexible as you get older and you've probably got to fit the ironing in and a trip to the garden centre, so you can't mess about with the wheelbarrow position ...'

'I'M GOING OUT!'

'SON! I'M JUST TRYING TO TELL YOU THAT NO WOMAN WANTS A PENIS IN HER EAR, THAT'S ALL!'

Don't worry: we will be having these conversations and they're going to know what women do and don't like. As a gay woman, I can offer that gift to my children, even if it means sitting down and watching porn together as a family.

'OK, I'm going to pause it here. Can you see what he's doing with his penis? He's just randomly slapping her vulva with it. I know she looks like she's enjoying this, but trust me, she's really thinking about whether or not she needs to buy some milk on the way home. Also, never knead a woman's breast like you're trying to make pizza dough ...'

I know what you're thinking.

'Jen, this is very heteronormative of you, what if your sons are gay? Or trans? Sex will be very different.'

You're absolutely right, but don't worry, I've thought of that too, and I think the principles remain the same, as does the message, which is this:

'Your penis isn't magic: orgasms don't happen by waving it about.'

It's a strong message and I can't wait to spread the word.

20

Looking Back

As you can probably tell by now, I don't shy away from being brutally honest. I think the funniest humour comes about when you can break down pretence and convention and reveal the painful, all-too-human truth at the heart of almost any subject. I also think it is helpful to tell the truth, or *your* truth, about the day-to-day reality of bringing up kids. As I've said, no one size fits all when it comes to parenting, and everyone's story is going to be different, but for most of us, I suspect, it's not perfect, we are not perfect, our kids aren't perfect all – or even some of – the time. So, what none of us need are those Instagram-perfect parenting stories on our social media feeds as a punctuation to the shitshow of actually bringing up small kids.

I will admit that being the 'other mother' did bring little bouts of neurosis at unexpected moments. When the kids were first born, I rarely referred to them as my sons. I thought of them as my sons, they ARE my sons; I just didn't say it out loud. Whether this was conscious or subconscious I'm not sure, but I seemed to find myself always referring to them as 'my boys'. It's not like I didn't feel a connection to them, I absolutely did. It wasn't a question of how much I loved them, or even my commitment to them; it wasn't because I had an issue with the biology of it, but something was holding me back.

Imposter syndrome AGAIN?

No one was making me feel insecure about my role as their mum: not Chloe, not her family, not my family, nor anyone we've met. This was all in my head – and because it was *in my head*, I didn't talk about it, or try to work it out by articulating it.

In some ways, this feeling about being the 'other mum', I realise, was not really about how I feel about them, I guess it was my worries about how they felt about me.

Before they were born, I used to joke that I was worried I wouldn't like them. 'If that happens,' I used to say, 'can we shove them back in and get another two?'

Despite, or perhaps because of my ever-present imposter syndrome, I'm a competitive person. Perhaps

I've had to be: if one part of your brain is constantly telling you that you are a fraud and you don't deserve to succeed, then you have no choice but to go out and prove to the gremlins on your shoulder that not only can you do it, but you can be better than everyone else on the bill.

One of the biggest motivators for me to continue with anything is to prove to myself that I can do it. I will take any amount of rejection and humiliation (I'm still talking about stand-up here) if I can eventually get to the point where I can achieve the very thing that I believe to be impossible. What can I say? I'm a complicated woman who would clearly benefit from a couple of decades of therapy.

As one of two mums, I'm not competing with Chloe; I can't compete. I understand that the relationship I have with my sons is different to the one that Chloe has. We are each offering something different, and together we make a great team for our children. Nevertheless, I still have those niggling voices telling me that I'm not their real mum, that I don't deserve them. So, I do what I always do: I dig deep and I give my everything to prove to myself that I do deserve them and that I AM their mum, albeit the 'other one'.

My sons can be as clingy with me as they are with Chloe, we have a strong bond and I know they love me. They're at their happiest when we are both around but when either of us has to spend time away from them, they are perfectly happy with whomever is left.

Chloe's relationship with our sons is different than mine: she was so natural with them when they were babies, she picked them up and somehow placed them in the exact spot on her body where they felt instantly safe and warm, whereas when I held them at first, I sometimes felt it was a bit awkward and clumsy. I felt that I had to work harder at making a connection that seemed to just be there for Chloe.

It's OK to acknowledge there's a difference between Chloe and me – that doesn't weaken my relationship with my children or with Chloe. I believe, that as far as my sons are concerned, all they know is that they have two parents, two mums. They love us both and in their eyes our roles are very clear to them.

I'm Mama and Chloe is Mummy.

Chloe and I talked about what the boys were going to call us early on. Apart from anything else, it could cause confusion to have two Mummies in the house at the same time, so I said I would give myself a different parent name than Mum. Picking a name for yourself as a parent is a weird thing to do. If you're hetero, of course, there is no question of who you are and what your children will call you. You don't have to sit with your partner and work it out: 'OK, so we've got Mama, Mummy, Mum, Mom, Momma,

MiMaw, Mum-Mum, Mother, Madre, Mam, Mama-Jen, MummyJen, MumJen & MJ ...'

It's a bloody minefield, and for those of you who think it's hilarious to suggest the name 'Mad' because it's a mixture of Mum and Dad, trust me when I say it's a lot funnier in your head.

So, my sons have a Mummy and a Mama and there is nothing weird, or confusing, or out of the ordinary about this to them because this is all they know. What I know is that, yes, in the conventional sense of the word, I am not their mum, and I am not their dad: but I *am* their parent. And yes, I feel fortunate to be the 'other' parent AND a gay woman, because I don't have to adhere to any societal expectations of 'motherhood'. Chloe and I have the huge joy and privilege of being our sons' parents, but we get to set the parameters and do it our way, the very best way that we can. *Vive la* matriarchy!

I'm bewildered and saddened and, yes, angry, when I hear that some people still have a problem with gay people becoming parents. The idea seems to be that if you are gay, you are somehow deviant. Yes, we deviate from whatever is considered the 'norm' – but the difference ends there.

Gay parents are doing the same job that all parents are; bringing up their children with love. We don't spend all day trying to indoctrinate our children into being gay. As I've said before, that is not something we have ANY CONTROL over. Our sons are not being forced to watch Judy Garland movies on a loop, dressed in gold lamé evening gowns, while lip-syncing to Lady Gaga.[1]

More than twenty years since Section 28, the idea that gay visibility and equality is something that needs to be feared, continually questioned and debated, is depressing and frustrating for LGBTQI people everywhere. Education is the key, and the earlier we start bringing the conversation about LGBTQI out of the dark ages and into the bright light of the twenty-first century, the better, as far as I'm concerned. Rather than schools avoiding the subject, homosexuality needs to be discussed. A conversation *can* and *needs* to be had, even with primary school children, that some people have two mums or two dads and their heads won't explode with the horror of it all.

On a personal level, any lingering qualms about not being their mum are never going to run very deep. My kids never fail to set me straight on that front, because nothing has brought me as much pleasure in the entirety of my middling life than hearing my sons call/shout/yell/snarl/moan/whine and whisper, 'Mama'.

---

[1] Once a year, sure.

I don't know why I was so surprised to hear them call me that as I had spent the entirety of their lives referring to myself in the third person to really drum it into their tiny heads.

'Mama loves you.'

'What did Mama say about putting stones in your mouth?'

'Mama doesn't like it when you bite her.'

I imagine it's as irritating to hear out loud as it is to read. Does everyone do this, or is this just the insecure workings of the 'other mother'? Answers on a postcard please.

Just be grateful that my third person references haven't stretched to adult conversation: 'Jen's really tired.' 'Jen's just popping to the shops.' 'Yes, Jen would love another drink.' I think we can all agree that it wouldn't be long before someone rightfully dashed my drink in my face.

Of course there have been times when my sons have made it clear that I wasn't the one they wanted when they called, or when they've demanded to be with Chloe and not me. On the whole, I have always been fine about this, sometimes I confess it has stung a bit, but you can't really get upset with a baby. It's not like they never asked for me, it's more that when they didn't want me, boy did they make that obvious. They're acting on impulse and have no idea that anything they say or do might affect your feelings. As I've explained, they are basically empathy vacuums.

Sometimes I get it completely, more recently now that they are four – it can be galling when you walk into their bedroom in the morning only to have one of them scream in your face:

'NOT YOU! I DON'T WANT YOU! I WANT MUMMY'

Don't get me wrong. It's not all bad. This has definitely worked to my advantage as I crawl back into bed at 6am.

'He doesn't want me, he wants you.'

Other times, it's just bloody annoying. It's a tricky time when your son or daughter rejects you, not just once but over and over again. I often think that one of these days I'm going to sit them down and say:

'Look, you need to wind your neck in because you're stuck with me. Yes, me. The other one. The one that was up all night almost every night for the first twelve months of your life rocking you to sleep, changing your nappy, sucking snot out of your nose so you could breathe – yeah! Guess what, your mum refused to do that – took you out for five a.m. walks in your buggy in the freezing cold and rain while you were cosy in your sleeping bag and waterproof cover, sometimes for over two hours just so your mum could sleep, spent hours making you pureed food that you would throw at the wall, stood in a playground for hours, bored out of my mind trying to avoid eye contact with other mums, yeah I'm that mug. So, let's go downstairs, I'll warm you some milk and we can both collapse on the sofa and watch *Paw* bloody *Patrol*, OK?'

If, for reasons that seem to make no sense to you, you are sometimes the less popular one, let me just say I feel your pain and reassure you that it doesn't last. And even though kids can be absolute bastards, they do love you.

It also helps to know that however neurotic/insecure/sad you might be feeling about your relationship with your child, as with most things, they will wake up one morning and surprise you by singling you out as number one. Relationships aren't static, they grow and change as we do and babies and children will form a stronger attachment to one of you at different stages in their life. And as other parents will know, it's not always the mum or the biological parent that has the stronger connection: children are fickle little buggers.

Once you hear your children calling you Mum, or Mama, or Dad or Dada, or whatever the bloody hell it is your kids call you, your heart will melt and you'll put up with almost anything. Including your son screaming, 'NOT YOU! NOT YOU! NOT YOU!'

In many ways, that is what being a parent is all about. Working tirelessly with no sleep, no thanks, no physical reward other than a smile or a hug from your child, if you're lucky. If you're unlucky, then it's a plate to the head, an exploding nappy, a four-hour non-stop tantrum, another sleepless night, a series of never-ending rejections ...

Good times.

But even that isn't the whole story, because every parent knows that if you're really, really lucky, you will have a child who is healthy and happy. Everything else is just gravy.

Our sons are now four years old. They are a delightful, exhausting, hilarious, frustrating, joyous pair of lovely lads whom Chloe and I adore. Four years in, and things have gotten so much easier now, in some ways. They can play together, which takes the pressure off both Chloe and myself. They can spend entire mornings entertaining themselves, making up games together or playing with Lego. Both of them love being outdoors and can spend hours climbing, scooting and generally mucking about. They are at an age where if we wanted to go away for a night, we could leave them with their grandparents without having to panic that they will miss us too much.

In other ways, there are new challenges to face. As same-sex parents, lots of people think the biggest one is having to explain why they don't have a dad (or, in the case of gay dads, a mum). Well, for us, it was easy:

'Mama, we don't have a dad, do we?'

'No, darling, you don't, you have two mummies.'

'Joanie doesn't have a dad either, but Joey does.'

'Yes, that's right.'

'And Ted and Arlo only have one mummy.'

'Well, some children have a mummy and a daddy, some have two mummies or two daddies, we have friends who just have a mummy or a daddy, don't we? Everyone is different.'

'Yeah … Mama?'

'Yes, darling?'

'Can you get the Lego out for me …?'

I imagine we're going to have to go into a bit more detail at some point sooner or later, but so far, so good. Even if they do ask tricky questions, we have all the answers for them, so I'm not in the least bit worried. The problems we have with our two boys are the same problems that every parent encounters.

Take bedtime. What used to be (at least for a while) quite a straightforward process of getting them to go to sleep[2] has more recently become a battle of wills. Their reasons for not being able to go to sleep range from needing another cuddle, to feeling hungry,[3] to wanting another story, to needing a poo. I'm beginning to think

---

[2] I'm not saying they stayed asleep, but at least we had a couple of hours' grace.

[3] Well, you should have eaten your bloody dinner then!

my children can poo at will, because the 'I need a poo' excuse is used a lot and weirdly always ends in a poo, which is frustrating when you're trying to tell them that they're lying and they then spend the next twenty minutes laying cable.

The little one in particular is really honing his negotiation skills, I'm assuming for when he picks up a job at the UN:

'Mama, I will go to bed if you read me another story.'

'No, that's not how this works. You've had two stories already so now it's bedtime.'

'But if you want to, you can read us a story while we're in bed.'

'I don't want to. I want to go downstairs and have my dinner.'

'WELL, IF YOU DON'T READ ME A STORY, I WON'T BE YOUR FRIEND FOR A HUNDRED YEARS!'

'Sure, OK. Night-night then.'

I'd like to tell you that's where the nightmare ends, but that's just the start of a two-hour saga involving them jumping off each other's beds: 'GET INTO BED! Now!'

Switching on whatever light they can reach: 'TURN THE LIGHT OFF NOW!'

And creeping down the stairs to hide behind the sofa: 'I know you're hiding behind the sofa! GET TO BED RIGHT NOW! PLEASE!'

They also have numerous opinions on things they didn't give a toss about just six months earlier. For example, opinions on what they're wearing:

'Can I wear my Santa Claus jumper?'

'It's June, so I think we should save it for December when it's Christ ...'

'I WANT TO WEAR IT TODAY! PLEEEEASE, MAMA!'

Fine! Wear a thick viscose-cotton mix Christmas jumper in June. Knock yourself out!

They also don't seem to listen to a bloody word either of us say. Our days are spent talking in repetitive circles:

'Can you eat your breakfast?'

'Put your shoes on, please.'

'No toys to be taken out of the house.'

'There is no telly today, you watch enough TV ...'

'Can you please put your shoes on!'

'No, you can't have a biscuit.'

'Eat your broccoli, please. Look, it's like eating a tiny tree!'

'Don't hit your brother! I don't care if he has an annoying face.'

'WILL YOU PUT YOUR BLOODY SHOES ON RIGHT NOW BEFORE I COMPLETELY LOSE MY RAG!'

They can be really bloody annoying.

But then out of the blue they'll walk over to you, put their tiny little hand in yours, look up at you and say:

'I love you Mama.'

And you forgive them EVERYTHING.

Epilogue

These days Chloe and I have more downtime to actually take a breath, have a grown-up conversation, reflect on this or that. Strangely, though, even though we have this headspace, the kids are still our main topic of conversation. We're just not the same people we were before kids.

It can be nice to look back over the years since the boys were born and congratulate ourselves for holding our shit together during this crazy time. But when we recall the last four years, I sometimes wonder if Chloe's had some kind of lobotomy when I wasn't looking:

'It wasn't that bad, Jen! I really miss them being babies ... .'

'I'm sorry but WHAT?'

'They were just so small, I miss being able to pick them up and carry them around the house with me.

I miss their little fat feet and having them fall asleep on my chest ...'

'Do you? DO YOU REALLY? Do you also miss getting up every hour and breastfeeding them, do you miss not having any kind of life because we couldn't leave them with anyone, do you miss leaving the house with a rucksack previously used for when you went camping?'

'Yeah, I do really ...'

I don't. I love my boys very much but I do not miss the baby bit and I do not wish to go back there ever, ever, ever again. I see mothers with babies and I just think:

'You poor bastard.'

Whereas Chloe looks at mothers with babies and thinks:

'I wish we'd had another one.'

That's what hormones do to you. They can make you think that you want another baby. Surely that can be the only reason why parents go through hell, get out the other side of it and think:

'Yeah, I want to go through that again.'

We talked about a third baby, not long after the twins. It was a conversation that we needed to have, because we still had two embryos on ice. The clinic had written to us and we needed to decide if we were going to keep them, or not.

I did not want another baby, BUT I also wasn't ready to say goodbye to our potential babies. Consequently, the circular conversation of whether we would have another one started when our boys were only a month old.

We avoided that letter for months, which was hardly surprising given that we were just about coping with looking after our two newborn babies. A second letter arrived from the clinic a couple of months later, we avoided that one too, as you do when you want to sidestep any kind of decision. It was only four months after the first letter arrived, demanding payment or they would destroy our embryos, that we knew we weren't ready to say goodbye to them. We paid up.

We paid the following year and the year after that, all the while discussing how our lives might change if we had a third baby:

'You could only work weekends again.'

'We'd need a bigger car. In fact, we'd probably need a bloody van.'

'We wouldn't be able to afford to go on holiday.'

'You'd have to give up your office so we could make it into a bedroom.'

'I don't think I want a third kid, do you?'

'God no.'

Fast-forward three months.

'What do you think about having a third one?'

This went on for THREE YEARS.

Every couple of months, we'd go through the pros and cons of having a third child. Honestly, if Chlo had desperately wanted to have another baby, I would have gone with it. I am, however, very glad we didn't because I think if we had, I'd probably be but a shell of the shell of a woman you see before you today.

I don't know how people cope with three kids. I don't know how my mum coped with four children under the age of six. It just sounds miserable and it makes no sense to me. The work that goes into looking after two children is enough – chuck in a third and we wouldn't just be out of our depth, we'd be full-on out to sea and drowning.

Maybe if I had been younger when we started this whole process, I might have considered it. But I was thirty-nine when the boys were born and I have a lot less energy as I head into my forties than I had in my early to mid-thirties. Also, knowing what we'd have to look forward to, I couldn't go through it again. People have tried to reassure us by letting us know it's different when you just have one baby. Maybe it is different, but I've met enough parents with one baby who look broken to know that isn't necessarily the case.

The people who are most keen for you to have a third baby is always your mate who has three kids:

'Honestly, it's the best thing we ever did, at the time, it didn't feel like it, did it, Dave? But now they're all at secondary school we're so glad we've got three.'

'What about the first eleven years?'

'Well, yes, they were tricky, but that's because we were separated for two of them ... .'

No thank you.

We're very lucky, we have two healthy, happy children. We're not naive, we understand that illness and disability can strike an individual at any time, but it felt like tempting fate to have another baby. To me, and particularly as we hadn't adopted a child, it seemed almost greedy to want a third when there are so many children who are already here and desperately need a home.

You won't be surprised to hear that we are happy to settle on two. Who knows, we might foster or adopt in the future, we've discussed it and it's a possibility, but for now these two lovely lads are more than enough for both of us.

It still felt weird to say goodbye to those embryos. I would have been happy to pay to keep them for another year. I don't know why. As security? Or maybe because I have so much love for our sons that I wonder who those unborn children might have been. Who can say if Chloe would have even got pregnant again, but when we finally did decide to let them go, we both felt a pang of regret afterwards.

I'm sure that's normal, but a year on and I know we made the right decision. Even if, after looking back at photos of our boys as babies, we have the occasional nostalgic moment, there is no way either of us want another child.

They say you should know your limits and I think it's fair to say we've hit ours.

I am forty-four years old. Forty-four. I live in a house in Brighton with my long-term girlfriend, Chloe. We have been together for thirteen years but we're not married. I am earning a decent wage as a professional stand-up comedian. I am no longer pretending to be young. I am forty-four years of age. Forty-four. I have some savings and better career prospects. I take my responsibilities seriously. I am happy in the path my life is taking. I am a mother to twin four-year-old boys whom I love with every fibre of my being. I have learned a lot since becoming a parent. I have learned that I am not just Other.

I am a mother.

Acknowledgements

I'd like to thank my dear friend and life coach, Francesca Martinez for badgering me for YEARS to write this book (Look I've done it, Chess!), to Kevin Hely for telling me I could do it and to all the Martinez family for always being there for me. To Judith Quin for helping me start this book and reminding me where the beginning really is. To David Jordan for being my creative go-to, friend and confidant and Cathryn Wright for being my good friend and second publicity team.

Thank you to Hannah Gadsby and Viv Groskop for helping me with my proposal and giving sound advice and encouragement. Emma Freud for her insanely positive feedback. To Sara Pascoe, Sarah Millican and Shappi Khorsandi for their constant support, and Frankie Boyle and Romesh Ranganathan for being such good mates. To Deborah Frances

White for giving me a brand-new platform to show off on and to my partner in crime Maureen Younger for having to listen to me endlessly moan about deadlines, you are a true friend. To Suzi Ruffell, Kerry Godliman and Zoe Lyons for always picking up the phone, Mickey and Hannah and all the *Standard Issue* gang, this book would not be in existence without you.

Huge thanks to my literary agent Cathryn Summerhayes for believing I could write this and to Hollie Ebdon who has been the best thing to happen to my career in over a decade. I am indebted to my editor Rowan Yapp and also to Harriet Dobson, Lucie Cuthbertson-Twiggs and my copy-editor Rose Davidson who helped me turn my ramblings into an actual real-life book!

To people who have helped, supported and championed me on the way, I wouldn't be here without you: Della Hadingham, Charlotte Austin, Flo Collins, Linda Riley and John Noel.

To Alyssa and Carly for getting me on the BYOB train and for all your support with my book.

To my friends you are too many to mention because I am so popular,[1] but you know who you are and I love you ALL dearly. To Lucy Drake who left us

---

[1] Not really, I'm just worried I'll leave someone out.

too soon and whom I miss every day, to the Brighton Massive: Trak, Diana, Becks, Neil and Meg and all the sprogs and to Sian for being a bloody hero. To my NCT gang, all of you are an 'inspiration' to me! To my comedy mums: Jess Fostekew, Katie Mulgrew, Hatty Ashdown, Sara Barron and The Shirleys. KEEP GOING YOU CAN DO IT! Also to Jeremy Hardy who I loved and miss greatly and who would no doubt have hated reading this book. And to all my comedy mates on the road, you know who you are! I thank you for your camaraderie, friendship and heavy-duty schadenfreude, I expect you all to buy the audiobook and listen to my voice in the car as you drive to Cardiff/Newcastle/Glasgow/Manchester/Norwich...

To Charlotte Baker, you didn't get a mention in the book, but I don't want you or Della to think you were forgotten, WE LOVE YOU!

To Rosemary for her kind words and to Ange and Jon for being the best in-laws a person could ask for. To Liz and Richard for EVERYTHING and to Jude and Chris, Matthew and Siwan for welcoming me into the family. Also, to the rest of the Martin-Houghton-Ball-Gibson clan, I've enjoyed being ribbed endlessly by all of you.

I want to thank my brothers Alex, Greg and Stephen who have always laughed at my jokes and to remind them that I love them. If you forget, please read this back to yourself ad infinitum. To my Mum for being my constant rock and number one fan, I love you very much and last but not least, to Chloe and our two lovely sons. You are the inspiration for this book, please don't hold it against me.